A HISTORY OF
HUNTING
IN THE
GREAT SMOKY
MOUNTAINS

BOB PLOTT

FOREWORD BY GEORGE ELLISON

THE
History
PRESS

Published by The History Press
Charleston, SC 29403
www.historypress.net

Cover image: *The Station Camp — Dogs and Deerskins* and inside illustrations courtesy of H. David Wright, artist of the American frontier. His work can be viewed at www.davidwrightart.com.

First published 2008
Second printing 2010
Third printing 2011
Fourth printing 2012

Manufactured in the United States

ISBN 978.1.59629.458.5

Library of Congress Cataloging-in-Publication Data

Plott, Bob.
A history of hunting in the Great Smoky Mountains / Bob Plott.
p. cm.
Includes bibliographical references.
ISBN 978-1-59629-458-5
1. Hunting--Great Smoky Mountains (N.C. and Tenn.)--History. I. Title.
SK43.P56 2008
799.29768'89--dc22
2008031397

This book is dedicated to my late father, P.G. "Shine" Plott, and to my late uncle, Cecil Plott, both of whom instilled in me an undying love of the Great Smoky Mountains—a place that I consider home.

"I always was somewhat of a fool about the woods. I live in them, just because I love them. When I was young they wasn't nothin' about the mountains I didn't want to learn, and they wasn't no risky thing that I didn't want to do!"

—Smoky Mountain hunter "Black" Bill Walker speaking to author Robert Mason in the early 1900s

CONTENTS

FOREWORD

It sometimes seems that certain people are born to write books. That appears to be the instance with regard to *The Story of the Plott Hound: Strike & Stay*. Published by The History Press in 2007, the book begins in the mid-1700s when the original breeder, Johannes Plott, sailed from Germany to America with little else but several prized dogs. In time, the Plott family perfected the breed as they moved westward in North Carolina into the Great Smoky Mountains region.

In retrospect, it does appear that Bob Plott, the great-great-great-grandson of Johannes Plott, was destined to unveil for the first time the interrelated story of his family's history and legends. But just as significant, in the long run, is the fact that Plott himself is an accomplished outdoorsman and hunter with considerable knowledge of Cherokee and pioneer history. All of these factors converged to transform *The Story of the Plott Hound* from a family history into a regional saga of lasting significance.

A History of Hunting in the Great Smoky Mountains is the logical and perhaps inevitable sequel to Plott's first book. Herein, he has broadened his prospective to craft an overview of the history of hunting methods and equipment in the mountains of Western North Carolina and Eastern Tennessee, especially the region centered upon the more than 500,000 acres that were incorporated into the Great Smoky Mountains National Park in 1934.

Within that framework, he has provided informative and often humorous biographical sketches of many of the region's more famous hunters, dog breeders, rifle makers and often outrageous characters, ranging from the time of the earliest Cherokees to the present: Kanati, Russell Bean, John Gillespie, Samuel Click, Fredrick "Uncle Fed" Messer, Israel "Wid" Medford, Montraville "Mont" Plott, George "Turkey George" Palmer, William "Black Bill" Walker, Wiley Oakley, Garland "Cotton" McGuire, Will Orr, Acquilla

"Quill" Rose, Mark Cathey, Samuel Hunnicutt, Granville Calhoun and many others.

Plott's detailed rendering, in the context of the "man hunting" tactics (allegedly involving cannibalism) of several Cherokee warriors during the eighteenth century, will no doubt be controversial. On the other hand, his depiction of the "man hunting" tactics of Marshall McClung, a master outdoorsman and tracker who locates individuals lost in the mountains, is inspirational.

Readers will be interested, I think, to learn that the author isn't just an armchair historian. When Plott describes the methods and equipment utilized by pioneer hunters, he knows exactly what he is talking about from direct experience as a founding member of Gist's Company of Scouts. This is a group of like-minded souls who seek to push the envelope and actually recreate, insofar as possible, the lifestyles and conditions faced by eighteenth-century explorers and hunters. The name honors Christopher Gist, who lived in North Carolina as an Indian trader and hunter and fought in the French and Indian War with a group of scouts. Like Plott, many of the group's members are hunters who use only eighteenth-century weapons and gear. All are avid outdoorsmen who hike and camp in extreme conditions. All clothing weaponry and accoutrements must be fully documented as being period correct. All leather or hides are either brain tanned or bark tanned. They cook over open fires started by flint and steel and eat only period correct foods.

Plott tells me that he initially envisioned *Hunting History* as a compilation of brief character sketches depicting some of the region's legendary hunters. That would have been nice. But when he went a step further and opted to place those materials within their ongoing historical context, he has once again transformed them into a cultural overview of lasting historical significance.

George Ellison
Bryson City, North Carolina
June 2008

Acknowledgements

The first hardback book that I ever purchased was an autographed copy of *Mountain Bred* by John Parris. I bought it for $5.95 at Bennett's Drug in downtown Bryson City, North Carolina, in 1968. I was eleven years old. Then and now, the late John Parris is one of my literary heroes. There are several reasons for this—his crisp writing style, his love and knowledge of mountain people and mountain places, as well as the fact that he could actually make a living doing something that he truly *loved*. Ever since then my dream has been to find a way to do that myself. I haven't quite done it yet, but I'm getting there. And I have the following people to thank for their support, inspiration, input and guidance in helping me follow that dream.

George Ellison continues to be my mentor, editor, role model and friend. There would be no books by me without him. Like John Parris, George continues to be an inspiration to me. I am also grateful to him for allowing me access to his vast library.

To me, researching a project is the most enjoyable aspect of writing a book, and the good friends you often make while doing that research is icing on the cake. Some of the wonderful people whom I met working on his book are now valued friends. They include Mrs. Leota Wilcox, her daughter Vicki and her son Tommy, all members of the celebrated Denton family. All have become my dear friends, but Mrs. Wilcox and Tommy Wilcox deserve special mention for their detailed research assistance. Graham County man hunter and writer Marshall McClung not only has become a friend, but he also introduced me to a ninety-eight-year-old bear hunting legend, Mr. Dewey Sharp. What a treat it was to meet him!

It was truly my honor to finally meet Mr. and Mrs. Earl Lanning. I have my friend Dennis Glazener to thank for introducing me to this muzzleloading legend, as Earl Lanning is the "Godfather" of primitive black powder firearms. And Dennis is no slouch himself—his input on his ancestors, members of the gun-making Gillespie family, was invaluable to this project.

Special thanks go to Annette Hartigan, the librarian for the Great Smoky Mountains National Park, who patiently helped with research, made copies and provided cheerful access to the pictures and books in the park archives, and to Ann Moore, director of the Foxfire Foundation. Thanks also to writer Jim Casada for his input and photos.

I am particularly grateful to Ron Pinson, Harold Jerrell, John Booy, Katy Talbert, Charles Brown and David Wright for their photos and artistic contributions. Having a David Wright painting for the cover is a special honor.

Some "old" friends also deserve special mention. Plott dog historian, hunter and writer John Jackson has become one of my best friends. We covered many miles together researching this book, as well as other Plott dog–related projects, and he is always a joy to be around.

I experienced some difficult times in my professional life while working on this book and I want to offer special thanks to the following folks who supported me. Some already have been mentioned, but must be included again: Mike Pritchard, Daniel Whitener, Lynn Moretz, Jeff Crisp, Charles Brown, Mike Alton, Mark Baker, Bill Carter, John Jackson, Frank Methven, Billy Chapman, Rick Davis, Harry Noel, John Young, Jerry Moody, Matt Mull, Ben Lilly and George Ellison are all men that I am *honored* to call friends. You guys are the best!

Last but certainly not least, I thank my family. My mother Mary has always been a supportive mom. But most of all, I thank my dear wife Janice for her tireless support, devotion and dedication. There has never been a better wife or mother, and she certainly deserves better than me. The same goes for my beloved son Jacob—a father couldn't have a better son. I have been incredibly blessed.

INTRODUCTION

For thousands of years, in almost all cultures around the world, people have firmly believed that no better hunters walked the face of the earth than those in their own respective countries. And whether it was in cave paintings or in verbal or written fashion, these hunters and their supporters all loved to share their stories. Some are true, while others are just tall tales. Some are funny, some are sad. A few even offer life lessons of sorts, but most of them are entertaining. Even as modern hunting has evolved into more of a sport than a means of survival, this remains true today.

Nowhere is this more evident than in the Great Smoky Mountains of Western North Carolina and East Tennessee. There is no question that there were, and are, many great hunting legends that have been told with gusto throughout the world for centuries. But for my money, the Great Smokies region is the hands-down winner when it comes to colorful, interesting hunters and hunting history.

Others areas throughout the United States, indeed even worldwide, certainly have their own classic hunting stories, but none can match or surpass those of this storied range. The legends here are twofold. The myths or stories alone are legendary in their own right. But so too are the often bigger-than-life individuals involved in these tales, who either were themselves the primary subject of these stories or who helped perpetuate them. And it was these almost mythical figures who defined the hunting history of the region.

However, it should be duly noted that while the bulk of this book is centered in the heart of the Great Smoky Mountains, I did take a bit of literary license to include a few stories in areas bordering them. But in all of these cases the characters or stories were tied directly to the region. I hope you enjoy these hunting legends and this hunting history of the Great Smoky Mountains.

CHAPTER ONE

THE ORIGINS OF HUNTING IN THE GREAT SMOKY MOUNTAINS

The Cherokee nation once ruled a kingdom of more than forty thousand square miles—almost seventy thousand square miles if you include areas that they considered their tribal hunting grounds. However, the heart of the Cherokee nation was and is in the Great Smoky Mountains of North Carolina. Indeed, the most sacred and original mother town of the Cherokee, known as Kituwah, is near present-day Bryson City, North Carolina, in the Ela community that borders the Great Smoky Mountain National Park. It was near here that the first Cherokee man, known as Kanati (the Lucky Hunter), and his wife Selu (Corn) first made their home.

The Cherokee referred to themselves as the *Yunwiya*, or "the real or principal people." Their culture was based on a simple sense of balance known as *duyuktv*, or the "right way." Basically, the tribe believed that there had to be a careful balance in all aspects of their daily lives. The men were expected to hunt, fish and fight, if need be, to feed and protect their people. The women farmed, cooked and took care of the children, along with other duties around the village.

But the "right way" of life was more complex than just a simple division of labor. Another part of this balance was about taking and using only what they needed, both in hunting and foraging for native plants. They wasted nothing and utilized all the parts of any animal they killed. The hunters usually asked for blessings and sang sacred songs before their hunts, and later they gave thanks to both the Creator and the animal itself after the kill.

The Cherokee were renowned as skilled and resourceful hunters and fishermen. Though a humble people, they still enjoyed sharing stories of their hunting adventures and tribal legends. Many of their ancient creation stories or myths revolved around Cherokee hunting heroes and their battles with the sometimes supernatural creatures of their era.

Most of these stories had a moral or important point to make for future generations to learn from. Others were simply humorous tales told for pleasure. Many of them would have been lost or never publicly recorded were it not for the Irish scholar James Mooney. Mooney was sent to the Qualla Boundary in 1887 by the director of the Bureau of American Ethnology. A part of his mission was to study and document the plants of the Great Smoky Mountains and their relation to Cherokee foods and medicine.

Mooney did that and much more when a segment of his report to the bureau was first published in 1900. It later was released in its entirety and became better known as *Myths of the Cherokee and Sacred Formulas of the Cherokees*. This amazing body of work included the first written record of many ancient tribal stories, medicinal formulas and sacred songs. Even today, it is recognized as the definitive historical study of the tribe. It also includes some of the earliest Cherokee hunting tales and legends.

Mooney's most valuable sources of information were the esteemed Cherokee shaman known only as Swimmer and the respected tribal patriarch John Ax. Swimmer was more than fifty years old in 1887, spoke no English and still lived and dressed in the traditional tribal way. Ax, too, was a traditionalist and was more than eighty years old when he first met Mooney. As a boy, Ax had been a keeper of the fire for many ancient rituals and ceremonies and he knew much of the old ways. Both men were Confederate Civil War veterans, having served in the Cherokee Legion of Colonel Will Thomas. It was with their assistance that Mooney first learned of the original Cherokee hunter Kanati and his wife Selu. It is also where we will learn how the traditional Cherokee believed the sport of hunting first originated in the Great Smoky Mountains, as well as why the region can be so challenging and difficult to hunt in.

Swimmer and Ax told Mooney that after creating the perfect paradise for them to live in, the Creator then made the first Cherokee man and woman, Kanati and Selu. Mooney believed that their home place was near Pilot Knob, an area known today as the Shining Rock wilderness, not far from present-day Waynesville, North Carolina. The couple prospered here, living the "right way" in perfect balance and bliss. Their homeland was a paradise, devoid of any harmful pests such as rodents, insects or snakes. Better still, there was no sin or sickness in this wonderful place. It could easily be compared to the Garden of Eden in Christian beliefs.

The Creator had provided for the couple in every way, even arranging for their food to be provided for them in a simple but unique manner. Kanati's name means Lucky Hunter in English, and rightfully so, for no hunter has ever had a more fortunate situation than he did in those ancient times. He needed few of the skills and talents that we recognize and admire in later-day hunters. To provide meat for his family, Kanati only had to take his bow and travel to a nearby cave. Along the way he would stop and make some arrows for his bow. Upon arriving at the cave, he would roll the rock covering the entrance aside, and out would run a fat, juicy deer or a plump turkey for him to harvest. Kanati would quickly close the entrance to the large cave, kill the deer or bird, field dress it and return home.

The Creator had also provided a sort of magical storehouse from which Selu could obtain the corn and beans that her family enjoyed. She would enter the storehouse with a basket, and after uttering some sacred words, could fill it with an endless supply of these vegetables. The key to this utopian lifestyle was for the couple to use only what they needed. They were to waste nothing to ensure that their perfectly balanced life could be maintained.

Kanati and Selu soon had a son and they flourished as a family, living a balanced and happy life. However, trouble arrived one day when their son was playing near a stream and met a magical playmate who would later come to be known as Wild Boy. It was difficult for the adults to see Wild Boy, as he always ran away when they approached. But eventually with the help of their son, Kanati and Selu were able to capture and tame Wild Boy. Soon he became their adopted son. Kanati quickly determined that Wild Boy had supernatural powers and that he had originated from the blood of game that Selu had washed off at the edge of the river.

As the boys grew into young men, they often wondered how Kanati and Selu so easily produced meat and vegetables for the family. Kanati and Selu were very secretive when they left on their hunting and foraging trips. They always took special caution to ensure that they were not followed.

But both of them underestimated the magical powers of Wild Boy. Wild Boy convinced his brother to accompany him as he attempted to follow Kanati on a hunting trip. The boys secretly stalked their father as best they could until they realized that he was too skilled a woodsman to be tracked by mere mortals. Wild Boy then used his powers to change himself into a piece of bird down, and caught a passing breeze so that he could be blown onto his adopted father's shoulder.

Wild Boy in his spirit shape watched closely as Kanati stopped to make arrows. He then flew off Kanati's shoulder and returned to his human form to tell his brother what he had seen. Kanati, thinking that he was safe from being followed, let his guard down and the brothers were able to catch up to him as he approached the sacred game cave.

They watched in amazement as Kanati rolled back the rock and a large deer bounded out. He then closed the cave as usual and killed the deer. The boys could not believe their eyes. They quickly returned home ahead of Kanati, who was slowed by the burden of the dead buck. He had no idea that he had been followed.

Shortly after that, Wild Boy and his brother decided to go on a hunting trip of their own. They made two bows and stopped to make seven arrows on their way to the cave. Upon their arrival at the cave, they quickly rolled the rock from its entrance and a deer ran out, quickly followed by another and yet another. The boys in their excitement began shooting the deer, but they forgot to close the cave entrance. Soon a huge herd of deer stampeded from the mouth of the cave. The last of the deer eventually galloped out, only to be replaced by herds of other four-legged animals, all of them coming out so fast and in such a large volume that it was impossible to close the cave. Raccoons, foxes, panthers, squirrels, rabbits, elk and groundhogs—*every* four-legged wild animal now known to man *except* the bear—ran furiously from the cave. They were followed by screeching, squawking flocks of every kind of bird imaginable. The sky blackened and the ground thundered from the sounds of these animals running or flying from the cave.

The boys were overwhelmed and helpless to stop this onslaught of beasts and birds. They watched in awe as the world filled with an entirely new kingdom of wildlife. Animals were now free to roam as they pleased all over the mountains.

Kanati heard the ruckus and rushed to the cave. By the time he got there, all the animals were long gone. Kanati was outraged. He entered the cave, where he found four large clay jars with lids on them. He angrily kicked the jars. The lids flew off and the air and ground were soon covered with all types of pests—fleas, ants, bedbugs, lice, gnats and ticks, just to name a few. The insects swarmed on the boys, stinging and biting them profusely.

Mooney recorded that Kanati then screamed at the boys, "Now you rascals have let out all the animals, and after this when you want a deer to eat you will have to hunt all over the woods for it and then maybe not find one."

The traditional Cherokee believed that this explains why even today hunting remains such a challenging sport, with no guarantee of "making meat" or getting food for the cook pot. It also explains the origins of all those pesky insects and vermin that hunters have had to deal with for years as they scoured the woods looking for game trails.

When Wild Boy and his brother unleashed all the animals and birds upon the world, there was one missing—the bear. Mooney explains simply that the bear did not exist then. But he explains why, and he also describes how the bear was created in his classic book.

The Cherokee felt a strong bond to the bear, a special sort of reverence, because they believed that *yona*, their name for the bruin, descended from an ancient tribal clan. This clan, who were once humans, had decided that they would prefer the more natural wild life of the bear versus the stress and worry of everyday human existence.

The Creator granted the clan their wish and turned them into bears, which according to tribal lore is why the bear is the animal that most resembles humans. These humans/bears also promised their Indian brethren that as long as they lived the tribe would have a reliable food source. However, the Cherokee were told to never forget where this food source originated and to always treat it with reverence and respect. Mooney states that the tribe was further instructed, "When you yourselves are hungry come into the woods and call us and we shall come to give you our own flesh. You need not be afraid to kill us, for we shall live always."

As Arlene Fradkin emphasizes in her 1990 book *Cherokee Folk Zoology*, the Cherokee took this offer very seriously and often killed bears reverently, but with great enthusiasm. She states that on one hunt, a bear "was resurrected to its proper form from the drops of its own spilt blood." She adds that another bear "was allotted seven lives and was killed repeatedly by hunters until it finally died its last death." So while the tribe had a great deal of respect for their bear brothers, they hunted them with a passion, believing that they were a never-ending food source.

James Mooney also found out why the traditional Cherokee believed that the bear clan could never be killed out. He learned that the chief of this ancient clan of humans/bears was called White Bear, who lived high in the Great Smoky Mountains at a site known as *Kuwahi*, or Mulberry Place. This is near the head of Deep Creek, on what is now known as Clingmans Dome. This massive 6,643-foot peak straddles the North Carolina and Tennessee border, between Swain County, North Carolina, and Sevier County, Tennessee.

The traditional Cherokee believed that there was a magical lake in this area called *Atagahi*, or Gall Place, where wounded and dying bears could retreat to and be healed. This mystical lake was fed by many bold springs flowing from the nearby high cliffs. It was a very wide but fairly shallow body of beautiful purple water. All manner of birds—especially huge flocks of wild ducks and pigeons—flew above the enchanted lake and swam on its surface. Many types of fish and reptiles also inhabited the lake, and the shoreline was filled with the tracks of the many bears that had traveled there to be magically healed or reborn.

Injured bears wounded by hunters or wild animals would travel here from all over the mountains. The wounded or dying bruins would then dive into one side of the lake and emerge from the other side magically healed. Some Cherokee believe that the lake still exists today. Though the supernatural powers of the Creator had ensured that *Atagahi* could not be seen by human eyes, some tribal members also believe that the lake could be seen by a spiritual human who was willing to endure lengthy fasting and prayer.

Author John Parris and his friend, Cherokee bear hunter George Owl, describe it best in Parris's 1972 book *These Storied Mountains*. Owl told Paris:

> *When I was a boy the old men said that just because people can't see the lake was no reason to believe that it had dried up and disappeared. It was there they said. It would always be there.*
>
> *But only through fasting and prayer they said would any man ever see the Secret Lake and come to know its miraculous powers. To such a one the lake would appear at daybreak as a wide sheet of purple water fed by springs which gush from the crags about it.*
>
> *Of course some will argue that what would appear as a lake would be nothing more than one of the cloud lakes which fill the great voids below during the night and then rise when day comes.*
>
> *Sometimes after a rain when the clouds are below* Kuwahi *(Clingmans Dome) all the valleys seen from up above look like lakes. But who knows? Maybe one of these cloud lakes just could be* Atagahi.

Indeed. Who *does* know for sure? But thanks to James Mooney we have these, as well as many other classic Cherokee stories—many of them involving hunting—permanently recorded for our enjoyment. Moreover, we have the traditional Cherokee explanations of creation and how they believe that hunting, as we now know it in the Great Smoky Mountains, came to be.

CHAPTER TWO

THE EARLY CHEROKEE HUNTERS

Make no mistake about it—regardless of the creation theory that you personally subscribe to, be it religious or scientific, or whether you choose to dismiss the traditional Cherokee beliefs as simply myth—the Cherokee were exceptionally skilled hunters. Any true lover of the great outdoors will admire their skill sets, as well as how they lived their lives in harmony with nature, adhering to *duyuktv*, or the "right way."

Of all the animals hunted by these celebrated woodsmen, none were more important to them than the deer and the bear. The Cherokee particularly enjoyed eating venison, along with bear roasts, steaks and bacon. They used almost every part of these animals in some aspects of their daily lives. Hides made for fine clothing, moccasins, leggings, robes, blankets and pouches. The sinew was used for thread; bear gut was twisted into bowstrings. The antlers, bones, teeth and claws could be converted into tools, sewing implements, jewelry and ceremonial or decorative items. Even the fat of these animals was rendered into tallow, grease or oil for various uses.

The Cherokee hunted almost every kind of animal native to the mountains. Donald Davis notes in his 2000 book *Where There Are Mountains* that the tribe lived in the "ideal ecosystem for deer, elk, bear and buffaloes, as well as rabbits, squirrels, turkey and beaver." Davis further adds that the Cherokee not only avidly hunted these animals, but that they "also hunted groundhogs, rabbits, frogs, birds and turtles."

The Cherokee hunted big game such as deer, bear, elk and buffalo using their handmade bows and arrows. These bows were exceptionally strong. Spanish invaders in the early 1500s wrote that they were unable to even partially draw back the string of a Cherokee hunter's bow. The Spaniards also noted that the bows were strong enough to launch an arrow entirely through a horse from neck to hindquarters. Not only were the bows powerful, but the

Cherokee used them with extraordinary skill. A Cherokee warrior was able to accurately shoot six or seven arrows in the time it took the Spaniards to shoot and load their firelocks once.

The Cherokee crafted these simple but effective weapons from local hardwood trees such as hickory, locust or sycamore. The size and strength of the archer determined the specific size and pull of the bow, but they were seldom much more than three feet long. When the bow construction was completed, they were then soaked thoroughly in bear oil to enhance their flexibility and then slowly and carefully hardened over campfires. Bowstrings were made from stretched and twisted bear gut, or spun hemp. Once complete, the bows and strings received regular treatments of bear grease to protect both from dampness. The bows were always left unstrung except while in use.

Arrows were fashioned from lightweight mountain cane. Mountain cane is similar to river cane and bamboo, but is shorter in length and, as the name implies, grows in higher elevations than river cane. The tribe found that late fall was the best time to gather cane for their arrow production. These deadly projectiles were generally between twenty-eight and thirty-four inches long, depending on the space between the natural joints of the cane. The joints of the cane were rubbed smooth to improve accuracy and the stems were removed. When the shaft finally met the desired specifications of the craftsman, he would then carefully heat the arrow over a fire and get it as straight as possible by bending it to his satisfaction.

Razor sharp, hand-knapped flint arrowheads were then attached with either sinew or hemp. The Cherokee made and used two types of arrowheads: a round shouldered model attached with hemp for hunting, and a square, higher shouldered version attached with sinew for war. The reason for this was that the broader arrowhead attached with sinew would do more bodily damage, and the sinew would expand when mixed with human blood, making it more difficult to remove. But the rounder hunting arrowhead attached by hemp could be more easily withdrawn and used again.

Finally, to ensure straight and accurate flight, and to better balance the arrow, the hunter added feather fletching and nocked the arrow. The fletching usually consisted of two feathers that were attached either by using glue made from deer hooves or by tying them on with sinew. Some tribal historians maintain that hunters would sometimes dip the flint tips of the arrow in poison to make them even more deadly, while others dismiss this theory.

When hunting deer, the Cherokee sometimes used a whistle made by splitting a laurel twig and then inserting a small piece of wood in the cleft. Using this device, the hunter could mimic the sounds of deer and entice them closer to him. There are also early accounts from visitors such as John Lawson, Jean Bernard Bossu and Henry Timberlake of the tribe crafting "decoy" costumes made of deer hide, antlers and even eyes to look like a real deer. Dressed as "decoy" deer and using their whistles, these early hunters were able to get close to deer herds and "call them in" for an easier kill. So perhaps we should credit the Cherokee as being some of the first, if not *the* first hunters to employ the use of hunting decoys in the Great Smoky Mountains.

When they could not kill big game such as deer or bear with their bows, the Cherokee hunters often trapped them by using snares or wooden traps. In the early 1700s, with the coming of white traders, the Cherokee began to purchase or trade for steel traps, guns and tomahawks—implements that would make them even more productive as hunters and trappers, but that would ultimately also contribute to the demise of their "balanced" life of *duyuktv*.

For hunting smaller game, such as birds and rabbits, the tribe used only a blowgun and darts. The blowgun was the weapon that young hunters were first taught to make and use as children, and one that they often continued to use as adults. To practice and improve their skills, Cherokee children were taught to first kill grasshoppers with them. Once they could consistently kill grasshoppers in the wild, they were then allowed to graduate to small game.

American-born British army officer Lieutenant Henry Timberlake lived among the Cherokee people for more than three months in 1762, and he later escorted a tribal contingent on a visit to England. His book, *The Memoirs of Lieutenant Henry Timberlake*, first published in 1765, verifies the blowgun hunting skills of Cherokee children. Timberlake wrote:

> *There are a vast number of lesser sort of game, such as rabbits, squirrels of several sorts, and many other animals, beside turkeys, geese, ducks of several kinds, partridges, pheasants, and an infinity of other birds, pursued only by the children, who at eight or ten years old, are very expert at killing with a bacan* [blowgun] *or hollow cane through which they blow a small dart, whose weakness obliges them to shoot at the eye of the larger sort of prey, which they seldom miss.*

Arelene Fradkin writes that these blowguns were crafted from six- to eight-foot-long pieces of river cane that were carefully heated, straightened and fully hollowed for better accuracy. The darts were sharply pointed nine- to twenty-two-inch wooden slivers made from locust, white oak, red mulberry or hickory trees. They had thistle-down fletching attached with sinew to ensure accuracy, as well as to create a better air seal in the blow gun. Historian Charles Hudson believes that, contrary to popular belief, there is no physical evidence that tips of the darts were often poisoned with native plants to aid in their killing power. Hudson adds that the Cherokee hunters were deadly accurate with blowguns up to about sixty feet, and that the darts could easily penetrate the bodies of birds.

In 1988, John Parris interviewed Cherokee blowgun expert Hayes Lossiah, who was then eighty-three years old. Lossiah was a well-known mountain hunter, and he recalled hunting squirrels with a blowgun when he was twelve years old:

One time I remember back then, I took five darts and went into the woods to hunt squirrels. I was standing beside a tree and I saw a squirrel go into a hole in another tree. I stood there just as quiet as I could be. I didn't move, I just kept my eyes on that hole in the tree. Well, after awhile that squirrel stuck his head out of the hole. Just stuck his head out and seemed to be listening. I raised my blowgun to my mouth and took aim and gave a good puff and shot that squirrel right in the throat. He fell out of the tree.

The skillful old hunter then offered these tips on hunting with a blowgun: "When you are hunting small game such as squirrels and rabbits and birds, you try to get as close as you can. Never more than forty feet away. You can kill at that distance, and farther it don't have as much power. And you can't be as accurate."

Lossiah finally pointed out the reasons why the blowgun was so efficient when used by a stealthy hunter: "If you miss hitting a squirrel or rabbit with your first dart, you can get off another shot without scaring away the game. A dart don't make noise either in flight, or when it hits the ground. Not like a rifle or shotgun, or even a bow. No noise."

By properly utilizing and conserving what the Creator had bestowed upon them, and by developing hunting weapons, implements and skills that were second to none, the early Cherokee hunters had indeed achieved their tribal objective of living the right and balanced way.

By the mid-1500s, the first Europeans came into Cherokee country. The armies of Hernando De Soto and Juan Pardo were the first step in the slow but sure disruption of the harmonious way of life for the Cherokee hunter and, indeed, the tribe as a whole. However, the tribe was able to repel these invaders and managed to maintain their lives of relative harmony until the late 1600s.

The Cherokee, painting by
David Wright.

The remote and rugged geography of the region, combined with the fact that in 1700 an estimated 30,000 Cherokee lived and hunted in these mountains, initially prevented negative European interaction with the tribe. By 1716, however, the Cherokee had begun to regularly trade their furs and hides with English, French and Spanish traders for woven cloth, metal tools, axes, trinkets, guns and whiskey. It is estimated that by 1740 more than 150 traders were doing business with the Cherokee. Many of these traders lived and married within the tribe.

As Donald Davis points out, the situation had deteriorated so badly by 1745 that the Cherokee Chief Skiagunsta wrote to the governor of South Carolina, complaining, "Our people cannot live independently of the English. The clothes we wear we can not make ourselves. They are made for us. We use their ammunition to kill deer. We can not make our own guns. Every necessary of life we must have from white people."

The era of the market hunter had now begun. And it would prove to be the beginning of the end for the right or balanced way of life of the Cherokee hunter and his family.

CHAPTER THREE

THE MARKET HUNTERS

It is a common misconception that market hunting, or hunting and trapping for profit, first began in the Great Smoky Mountains in the early 1700s when English traders began regularly doing business there. The fact is that market hunting began more than thirty years before that, when the Cherokee began to trade with the Spanish. However, due to the long distances involved to conduct this business and the almost constant hostilities between the two groups, the Cherokee never traded significant amounts of hides and furs to the Spanish. English seaports from Virginia to Georgia provided easier access for the Cherokee to trade and ship their hides. The influx of white traders visiting and even living with the tribe would further expedite the process. The fur trade grew so quickly that in 1716 a superintendent was appointed by the Crown to oversee these operations and regulate the European traders who were living and working among the tribe.

These traders and their overseers quickly developed a standard value system for trading pelts. Deerskins were the most common hide traded at the time. Donald Davis notes the value that the traders established on items that were most coveted by the Cherokee:

> *Rifle or musket: 35 deer hides.*
> *One yard of woven cloth: 8 deer hides.*
> *An axe or hatchet: 5 deer hides.*
> *30 rifle balls or bullets: 1 deer hide.*

Davis also adds that miscellaneous items such as salt, mirrors, gunpowder and kettles were in such great demand that "they fixed no price upon them, leaving the traders to exact as much as the savages were willing to pay for them." This, of course, only generated more bad feelings among the Cherokee toward the traders, and Europeans in general.

As the Cherokee became gradually more dependent on English goods, they began to rabidly hunt and trap animals to trade for what they wanted. It is difficult today to understand the devastating impact that this had on their hunting culture, as well as on the environment of the Great Smoky Mountains and the surrounding Cherokee hunting grounds. But consider these facts: between 1700 and 1715 more than one million individual animal hides were shipped from the port of Charleston, South Carolina; in 1753, over thirty thousand deerskins were traded and exported from the Rowan County district of the colony of North Carolina, not to mention an untold amount that were used by local native and white hunters of the area for clothing and moccasins; between 1755 and 1772 more than 2.5 million pounds of deer hides were shipped from the port of Savannah, Georgia.

Probably the greatest era in Cherokee fur trading took place between 1739 and 1761. It is only fair to point out that not all of these hides were obtained from just the Cherokee tribe alone. There were indeed other tribes involved in the fur trade, and even some white market hunters. Nor were all the hides traded in just Southern ports. But it is safe to say that a majority of these hides came from Cherokee hunters, as Donald Davis again points out:

> *In 1748 Charleston merchants are said to have exported to England 160,000 deerskins at an estimated value of 1.25 million dollars. In 1751 alone it was estimated that 100,000 pounds of deerskins were obtained by no fewer than two thousand Cherokee hunters. Four years later, Cornelius Doherty believed that if the winter season was favorable for hunting, he would be able to obtain 3,500 deerskins from his {trading} district alone. This would place the export figure for the entire Cherokee nation at approximately 25,000 skins. Assuming this rate held relatively constant between 1739 and 1761, it is conceivable that the Cherokees slaughtered well over half a million deer in this period alone.*
>
> *John Stuart, who kept yearly customs books for the Board of Trade, recorded a total of 5,239,350 pounds of deerskins leaving Charleston from 1739 to 1761. Depending on their size and age (older skins weighed slightly less, since weight was lost in the curing process) buckskins could weigh anywhere from 1 to 4 pounds. Using the later estimate, the Cherokee deer kill in the southern mountains for those years could have been anywhere between one and five million deer.*

Vast, almost unimaginable amounts of hides were harvested by Cherokee hunters during this time period. And while it is true that there were also

Market hunter C.S. Brown checks for Cherokee after deer kill. *Courtesy of Charles Brown.*

white market hunters actively involved in the fur trade then, the Cherokee—due to their growing dependence on trade goods—were their own worst enemies in bringing to an end the balanced life of the traditional tribal hunter in the Great Smoky Mountains. But, to be fair, unscrupulous traders, broken treaties and the terrible smallpox epidemic of 1738—all caused by the whites—had an even more devastating impact on the tribe.

By 1760, Chief Skiagunsta's 1745 lament to the governor of South Carolina had proven to be prophetic. The Cherokee tribe had become almost entirely dependent on European trade goods. The balanced "right way" of life for these tribal hunters was rapidly coming to an end.

Into the Woods, pencil drawing by
David Wright.

Big game such as elk and buffalo had already begun to diminish significantly in areas surrounding the Great Smoky Mountains by as early as 1770. In 1767, white market hunters reportedly killed more than seven hundred buffalo in less than two months. But because almost no one could safely hunt in the deep mountains except for the Cherokee—and despite the vast amounts of hides traded by the tribe—all sorts of wildlife, including elk, buffalo and even deer, continued to flourish here until the late 1700s.

It would remain that way until General Griffin Rutherford's "scorch the earth campaign" in the summer of 1776. The Cherokee had chosen to be allies with the British during the Revolutionary War and they had staged regular raids on frontier settlements for years prior to the war. Rutherford's plans were to brutally repay them for this mistake—and he did just that, offering little or no quarter to the tribe.

Rutherford, with more than six thousand men, most of them citizen soldiers or militia, completely destroyed more than thirty major Cherokee towns—almost the entire Cherokee mountain empire. Many Indian men, women and children were left homeless, and the skies were dark from the smoke of burning cornfields, orchards, homes and vast amounts of stored food.

Though the Cherokee would continue to fight for their homeland until 1794, this was the killing blow for the "right way" of life of the Cherokee hunter. But it would open the door for yet another generation of legendary hunters in the Smokies, as two different but similar hunting cultures fought for control of the Great Smoky Mountain region.

CHAPTER FOUR

MAN HUNTERS

Unfortunately, there is little documentation available regarding many of the Smoky Mountain hunting legends of the eighteenth century—especially when compared with the reams of information available on similar hunting cultures in Kentucky and middle Tennessee. But outside of oral tradition—and a few fine volumes by Henry Timberlake, William Bartram and James Adair—much has been lost over the years regarding the actual adventures of these eighteenth-century mountain hunters. And sometimes historians prefer to overlook the more brutal aspects of our hunting past.

Two legendary eighteenth-century Cherokee hunters were Doublehead and Bob Benge. While both were no doubt fine traditional hunters of wild game, it was another type of hunting—*man* hunting—that these two warriors are best known for.

Though the Revolutionary War ended in 1783, some Cherokee warriors continued to fight the white invaders until 1794. Unspeakable atrocities were committed by whites and Indians alike, with both sides vowing to avenge each senseless act of violence that had been inflicted upon them. As a result, a vicious cycle of man hunting began, with innocent parties on both sides paying a terrible toll for the evil deeds done by others.

Doublehead, or *Tsaluska*, was born in 1744 in the Overhill Cherokee Town of *Toqua*, near the base of the Great Smokies, in East Tennessee. As a young man, he quickly developed a reputation as a hunter and warrior. He was said to be a charismatic and courageous leader, but with an almost unquenchable lust for killing. Yet Doublehead was an extremely intelligent and articulate statesman, who later in his life used these attributes to gain great wealth. To describe him as simply a complex individual is an understatement of vast proportions. Perhaps this is why he was called Doublehead. He seemed to possess two wildly different personalities—one, a statesman and businessman able to live and thrive in the so-called civilized world, and the other side that of a brooding, homicidal maniac who often beat his wife and children. Perhaps some of this dark side can be attributed to the horrors that he had seen inflicted upon his own people, such as the brutal murder of his unarmed brother Old Tassel by a mob led by John Sevier. But certainly not all of it, as Doublehead was without a doubt a man who had an insatiable passion for man hunting.

In 1777, the Cherokee tribe split, with the faction that favored fighting the white invaders to the death becoming known as the Chickamauga Cherokee. They were led by the war chief Dragging Canoe. Doublehead soon became one of Dragging Canoe's most trusted lieutenants, and he led or participated in raids across the Southern frontier for almost twenty years.

On January 22, 1793, Doublehead led a raid into Kentucky, where his war party killed two white settlers and captured nine packhorses loaded with supplies. The warriors found whisky in their plunder and they decided to celebrate their kill. They soon became drunk. Doublehead suggested to his nephew, Bob Benge, and his brother, Pumpkin Boy, as well as the others in his group that they should try the old Iroquoian custom of "eating their enemy." Much to their dismay, he then began to cut strips of flesh from the white corpses and roast them over the fire. Doublehead considered this to be the ultimate insult to an enemy, and he believed that eating the heart or liver of an enemy would give him great strength. He ate the flesh and organs with great relish, and he finally convinced most of his comrades to partake in the bloody feast.

Late in 1793, as skirmishes continued in the foothills of the Great Smoky Mountains, the older Cherokee chiefs dispatched a delegation to discuss a peace treaty with President George Washington. Doublehead was among the members of this delegation. The president had heard rumors of Doublehead and his cannibalistic activities, and he asked the warrior if there was any truth to the story. Doublehead confirmed that the story was true. Washington then supposedly asked him which he preferred—the meat of wild game or that of humans. Doublehead wryly replied that he greatly favored the taste of wild game over that of humans, because "the meat of white men is much too salty."

Doublehead's alleged cannibalism, and his well-documented killing of an innocent baby in the summer of 1793, soon turned even seasoned warriors such as Bob Benge against him. And it was the baby killing, along with his later illegal sale of tribal lands, that eventually made him despised even among his own people and would lead to his death by tribal assassins in 1807.

A better and more honorable example of a Cherokee man hunter is that of Bob Benge. A good argument can be made that there never has been a more skilled man hunter in the Southern mountains than Bob Benge. He was born in about 1760 in the Cherokee town of Toqua. His father was a well-respected white trader named John Benge, who had lived among the tribe for years. His mother was Wurteh, a full-blooded Cherokee, who was the sister of the beloved Cherokee chief Old Tassel. Some sources say that she was also the mother of Sequoyah. If so, Benge and Sequoyah, who later created the Cherokee alphabet, would have been half brothers.

Though he was raised as a traditional Cherokee hunter with superb agility and stamina, Benge spoke fluent English and he physically looked like a white man, with his blazing red hair and fair skin. These skills and traits would prove invaluable to him as he grew into manhood and waged war on the whites. When he has seventeen in 1777, Benge and his family moved south to join Dragging Canoe and his Chickamauga Cherokee warriors at their village near what is now Lookout Mountain, Tennessee.

By 1785, Benge was a familiar and feared name across the frontier. As his legend grew, he became known by a variety of names, including the Bench, Chief Bench, Captain Benge and Chief Benge. Mothers in Virginia's white settlements were said to have told their misbehaving children, "You better be good or Captain Benge will come and get you."

In 1788, Benge saved hundreds of Cherokee lives when he helped evacuate and form a rear guard to defend against John Sevier's attack on the Cherokee village of Ustally. This town was located in the Great Smoky Mountains near the Hiwassee and Valley Rivers in southwestern North Carolina, not far from the modern-day town of Murphy. Sevier still managed to kill five Cherokee and burn the town, but he was turned back when Benge ambushed him near the mouth of the Valley River.

Between 1789 and 1792, Benge led scores of successful raids on white settlements across the mountain frontier, and the Virginia government placed a large bounty on his head. In the summer of 1792, Benge and his brother *Utana*, "the Tail," embarked on a man hunt for John Sevier. Cherokee citizens of Hiwassee Town reported that they had seen Benge and his brother, armed to the teeth, heading north with plans to kill their arch enemy. They searched for Sevier until early October, raiding several small settlements in the process before finally returning home empty-handed.

Late in 1792, Benge attacked a group of twelve white settlers that was traveling from Fort Southwest Point in northeast Tennessee to Nashville, Tennessee. Upon hearing the first shots, the seven white men in the party turned tail and ran, leaving four women and one child to fend for themselves

Tight Spot, painting by David Wright.

against the notorious Captain Benge. Benge quietly spoke to the terrified group in English and assured them that they would not be hurt or even taken captive. He built them a fire, rounded up their horses for them and then sent them safely on their way. Fortunately for them, Doublehead was not in this war party.

That was not the case in the infamous January 22, 1793 raid into Kentucky when Doublehead, Benge and Pumpkin Boy, among others, killed and allegedly ate parts of their victims' bodies. Though guilty of this horrible deed, Benge greatly regretted it and blamed it in part on his being intoxicated.

These two greatly contrasting incidents—one merciful, the other barbaric—would only further enhance Bob Benge's reputation as a man hunter on the Southern frontier. But it was his confrontation with Moses Cockrell in the spring of 1793 that would truly make him a man hunting legend.

Cockrell was a huge Virginian with quite a reputation as an Indian fighter. He had an even bigger reputation for drunkenly boasting in frontier taverns of his desire to fight Bob Benge to the death, one on one. Cockrell repeatedly vowed that he would be the man to personally see that Benge was punished for his atrocities.

He got his wish on March 31, 1793, when his party was attacked by Benge in what is now Lee County, Virginia. Benge had heard of Cockrell's boasts and was elated at the chance to fight him. He instructed his warriors to shoot the other two men in Cockrell's party but to leave Moses Cockrell for him alone. The raid was perfectly planned and Cockrell was indeed left alone to face Benge. Cockrell had a quick change of heart, fearfully dropped his weapon and sprinted away from Benge, with the red-headed Cherokee in hot pursuit.

Luckily for Cockrell, he was a much better runner than he was a fighter. Benge, armed only with his tomahawk, chased Cockrell for more than two miles to a remote cabin near Wallens Creek. Cockrell had barely managed to stay out of striking distance, but Benge, not knowing how many people were in the cabin, and with no rifle, made a last-ditch attempt to kill Cockrell by throwing his tomahawk at him.

Cockrell ran into the clearing around the cabin and jumped a fence just as Benge's axe struck the top rail of the barrier, barely missing his bulky body. Cockrell gasped for air as he found safety in the cabin and the settlers inside bolted the door. Benge stood out of rifle range in the nearby woods and taunted Cockrell to come out and fight. Cockrell wisely thought better of this and remained safely in the cabin. Benge finally retreated, leaving Moses Cockrell the laughingstock of frontier taverns for years to come.

For the remainder of 1793, Benge continued to raid white settlements on a regular basis, and he seemed to be particularly interested in capturing black slaves. In the spring of 1794, Benge schemed to steal every slave on the Holston River in Virginia before the end of the summer. On April 6, 1794, Benge began the first phase of his master plan when he raided the homestead of the Livingston brothers near Mendota, Virginia. The men were in the fields working when the attack began, enabling Benge and his party to easily capture the women of the house and their slaves. But Benge intentionally let the children escape to safety.

He then split his party, sending a small group ahead to hunt game. Benge and his rear guard followed behind with the prisoners, one of whom was Mrs. Elizabeth Livingston. After nearly two days on the trail home, Benge relaxed a bit and told Mrs. Livingston of his plan to capture slaves, especially those of the old Revolutionary War hero Isaac Shelby. She later reported that he seemed to be in grand spirits. Little did Benge know that a rescue party, led by the Livingston brothers and the Lee County militia, commanded by Vincent Hobbs, was hot on his trail.

Lieutenant Hobbs knew the country well and was able to ambush Benge's group near Big Stone Gap, Virginia. The ambush was perfectly executed by the whites and the Indians fell in a withering crossfire. Bob Benge, the scourge of the Southern frontier and its most famous man hunter, was dead at the age of thirty-five. No one knows for sure who killed him, but Vincent Hobbs claimed the scalp of the auburn-haired warrior and he was later rewarded for his efforts with a custom-made rifle from the governor of Virginia.

Raids would continue until the mid-1790s as John Sevier—one of the heroes of Kings Mountain—and other mountain militia men continued to wage war on the Cherokee. Sevier and many of his men were considered the man hunting equals of their Cherokee counterparts Doublehead and Bob Benge.

In 1778, while attacking the town of Hiwassee, a member of Sevier's militia named Thomas Christian brutally murdered a young Cherokee boy with the cold-hearted explanation, "Nits make lice." Another of Sevier's compatriots, John Kirk, formed a group known as the Bloody Rangers. Their sole purpose was to hunt and kill all Cherokee people. After his mother, wife and ten children were killed by the tribe, Kirk vowed to avenge them by hunting down any Cherokee in his path. His most callous murders were in June 1788 at the Cherokee town of Chilhowee, when he killed the unarmed Cherokee Chiefs Old Abram and Corn Tassel and two others while under a flag of truce.

This brutal cycle of man hunting continued until peace was finally achieved between the whites and the Cherokee at the Tellico Blockhouse treaty in 1794. With a final end to the Indian wars, the newly opened tribal hunting grounds would prove to be ideal for perpetuating the legend of the almost mythical old-time mountain hunters and their Smoky Mountain rifles.

CHAPTER FIVE

THE SMOKY MOUNTAIN RIFLE

The end of the Indian wars brought even more hunters into the Great Smoky Mountains, an area that remained still a wild frontier while lands farther west in Kentucky and Tennessee were becoming more populated and civilized. These early white hunters were a rough and hardy bunch, but they were very resourceful. They were of all races and creeds, but most of them were of Scotch-Irish, English or German descent. Many were veterans of the Indian border wars, Revolutionary War or War of 1812. Most were looking for a new home in the Great Smoky Mountains, while others were just transient market hunters looking to stay here only as long as they could make money hunting and trapping.

Regardless of their reason for being here or how long they intended to stay, almost all of these white hunters shared one unique skill—they were remarkable shots and they were masters of their muzzleloading flintlock long rifles. They could fire them accurately up to two hundred yards, while managing to get off three shots in about ninety seconds or less.

There is probably no more famous weapon in American hunting folklore or history than the legendary long rifle. Because of its association with Daniel Boone and other fabled frontiersmen of the "dark and bloody grounds" of Kentucky, it has become more commonly known as a Kentucky long rifle. That, however, is a misnomer, as the gun had its origins with gunsmiths from the Lancaster, Pennsylvania area, some of whom later moved south and continued their work in Virginia and North Carolina. Because of this, these firearms are often referred to as Lancaster rifles.

Building a quality hunting rifle, like crafting a Cherokee bow, was an art form. These classic metal and woodworking artisans were in great demand in the Southern mountains, so much so that by the late 1700s—and well into the late 1800s—there were several fine gun makers living in the Great

The Long Knife, pencil drawing by David Wright.

A Sound in the Stillness, painting by David Wright.

Smoky Mountains in both East Tennessee and Western North Carolina. These men became hunting legends in their own right by making a new variation of the Lancaster rifle. It would be called, appropriately enough, the Smoky Mountain rifle. It is a weapon that still remains a treasured piece of mountain hunting history and legend.

The Smoky Mountain Rifle

The Smoky Mountain rifle was a plain and functional gun. Unlike the Lancaster rifles, it had few frills, fancy carvings, inlays or other ornamentation. This was *not* due to ignorance or a lack of skills on the part of the mountaineer craftsmen. Far from it, for these were talented individuals. It was due to the demands and income of their marketplace. Simply put, there weren't many wealthy hunters living in the Smokies. Hunters were looking for an efficient and utilitarian weapon that they could afford, and the Smoky Mountain rifle perfectly fit the bill. As their reputation as artisans grew, and as their guns became more in demand, some of the gun makers did make their rifles more ornate and expensive. However, they pale in comparison to the elaborate earlier Lancaster guns.

Another unique feature of the rifle was its iron hardware, as opposed to the brass mountings on the Lancaster guns. Some have argued that this may have been because iron was cheaper than brass. Firearms experts like Wallace Gusler and Smoky Mountain gun maker Earl Lanning dispute this. Gusler states that brass was in fact cheaper then and that it was simply a matter of the mountaineer gunsmiths doing something differently and maintaining and perpetuating that tradition. Haywood County native Earl Lanning believes that it was also because iron was more easily accessible to the mountaineers, as it could be found and processed locally in mines and foundries.

The Smoky Mountain rifles seldom had metal patch boxes, but they sometimes had wooden ones. Most had no patch box at all, but instead had a simple tallow hole in the stock to store bear grease or tallow for patching, cleaning and lubrication purposes. Old-time hunters referred to this as a "taller hole."

Cosmetics aside, the secret to the success of both the Lancaster and the Smoky Mountain rifles was their hand-forged locks and barrels. All metal parts were, of course, hand forged back then, but it was the lock that ensured quick and reliable ignition when firing, and it was the long "rifled" barrels that made the accuracy of the rifles legendary.

Forging a barrel by hand is almost a lost art, still practiced by only a few artisans today. But on the Smoky Mountain frontier, most barrels were forged and rifled by hand, and it was a daunting task, usually requiring two men. Iron for the barrel was refined locally at a charcoal ore mine called a bloomery. It was then forged into a flat bar of wrought iron known as a bloom. Then the hard work began.

Once the barrel was hammered out flat to its desired length and width, the gunsmith heated it and bent it around a long rod called a mandril. He then welded the edges together a few inches at a time. Next, the barrel was heated again and buried in hot coals, where it was left to slowly cool and

Smoky Mountain rifle at a hunting camp; note the tallow hole in the stock. *Courtesy of Charles Brown.*

was later bored. Once bored to the desired caliber, the barrel was "rifled." Rifling, in its simplest terms, is cutting spiral grooves evenly spaced inside the barrel to force the lead ball to spin as it is fired, thus stabilizing its flight to ensure better accuracy. The rifling patterns were made by a tool known as a rifling guide. These varied depending on the caliber of the gun, the amount of the powder charge and the size of the ball. For example, a heavier powder charge and a lighter ball (bullet) required more twists or grooves.

Barrel making was grueling work done in difficult conditions, yet it required close attention to detail. Anything less would result in an inferior weapon. Over time, a heavily used hunting rifle would need to have its barrel refreshed when the rifling inside wore smooth. There were two ways to do this—both too complex to get into here—but basically the gunsmith had to re-rifle the barrel. This often changed the caliber of the gun from its original size, but it was cheaper than buying an entirely new gun or barrel.

The lock is a relatively simple firing mechanism that consists of a series of metal springs, rollers, tumblers and screws. Not only were these parts hand forged, but they also had to be carefully fire hardened to ensure longevity and reliability, and the moving parts were precision tuned like a fine watch. The locks were sometimes imported from England, but the mountain gunsmiths often made their own. The trigger and trigger guard, other iron hardware, hand-carved wooden stock and ramrod completed the Smoky Mountain rifle.

But even the best made locks and barrels were useless without gunpowder, ammunition and flints, and these resourceful mountaineer hunters had that covered too. The recipe for gunpowder is fairly simple—willow charcoal, saltpeter potassium nitrate, sulfur and stale urine, all ground together and then rolled out to dry in the sun. All of the ingredients were readily available in the Smoky Mountains. Alum Cave, near Mount Leconte, Tennessee, was first found by the Cherokee Chief Yonaguska while he was bear hunting in the early 1800s. The cave remained a primary source of potassium nitrate for Smoky Mountain hunters until the early 1900s.

Flints were plentiful throughout the mountains and were hand knapped by hunters to use in their flintlocks. A favorite "flint field" for hunters was the Equanulty Trace, or Old Spicewoods, as it was known by the Cherokee. The field was located near Cades Cove, Tennessee, and flints from here were said to produce a consistent "live, fat spark." The old bear hunter Chief Yonaguska valued them so much that on his deathbed he instructed his clan to either supply his corpse with an ample supply to carry with him on his trip to the afterlife or to bury him in his favorite flint field so he could supply himself.

1906 photo of young mountain hunter (name unknown). Note the old Smoky Mountain rifle and the size of the chestnut stump behind him. *Courtesy of Great Smoky Mountains National Park Archives.*

In 1822, the use of percussion-cap lock firing systems became popular, and many hunters either converted their flintlocks to cap locks or bought new guns. But flintlocks were still used until well into the early 1900s by many hunters, and some still use them today.

Lead for the balls (bullets) and for the iron hardware was also mined and forged locally. Large bars of iron were used by gunsmiths and blacksmiths for bigger projects such as gun barrels and tools. Small pieces of iron could be carried with hunters and melted into bullet molds for bullets that fit the caliber of their rifles. Often the hunters would dig bullets out of an animal and melt them to use again.

While the guns and accoutrements that these mountain craftsmen produced may have been considered plain and functional, the artisans themselves were anything but. Many of these gunsmiths are Smoky Mountain legends in their own right.

Some of the earliest and probably the most influential gunsmiths were members of the Bean family of East Tennessee. William Bean, a hunting partner of Daniel Boone and a veteran of the Battle of Kings Mountain, settled near present-day Jonesboro, Tennessee, in 1768, and he set up a gun shop there. It is not known where he learned his craft, but his family can be traced back to the McBean clan of ancient Scotland. Bean's rifles are generally believed to have been of smaller caliber than the Lancaster guns, equipped with the iron hardware and the basic no-frills style that are now trademarks of the Smoky Mountain rifle.

William and Lydia Bean's son Russell was born in 1769. He is believed to have been the first white child born in Tennessee. Russell carried on both the gun making and hunting traditions of his father. He was reportedly a big, muscular man, with dark hair and a black beard. Bean was said to have been extremely hot tempered and he was well-known for his fistfighting skills.

In the early 1800s, Russell took a load of his guns to sell in New Orleans. His initial plans were evidently to simply sell the rifles and take a long hunting trip on his return home. But Bean ended up staying in New Orleans for nearly two years, where he spent most of his profits on drinking, brawling, racing horses and cock fighting. When he finally got back home, Bean found that his wife had a baby that could not be his own. In a fit of rage, he cut off one or both of the child's ears to forever mark it as illegitimate.

Bean was later tried and convicted of the crime, and he was sentenced to be branded and jailed. Legend has it that it took several men to contain him when a mark was branded on the palm of his right hand to identify him as a criminal. After he was placed in a jail cell, Bean supposedly cursed his captors and *bit* the brand off his own hand to show his contempt for the punishment. Late that night he managed to escape from jail, but was later captured by a posse led by Andrew Jackson. Bean eventually was released after paying a heavy fine.

For all his flaws, Russell Bean was a gifted gunsmith. His guns sometimes had brass hardware and were known for their double patch boxes that were hinged in the middle. All of the Bean family rifles generally had a dark finish from a mixture of linseed oil and charcoal carbon to reduce glare from the wood or barrel while hunting in the woods. Other distinctive traits of the Bean Smoky Mountain rifles were a longer tang, which made for a stronger but thinner-wristed stock, and their uniquely designed trigger guards.

Bean family members, such as Russell's son James, as well as Charles, William and Baxter Bean, would continue their family legacy of Smoky Mountain gun making until the late 1800s. Many of the noted Smoky Mountain hunters of East Tennessee, such as George Powell and "Uncle" Sammy Burchfield, favored Bean rifles.

Another early Smoky Mountain rifle builder on the North Carolina side of the Smokies was John Gillespie. He, along with his three sons and their descendants, built fine mountain hunting rifles for almost a century, from the late 1700s to the late 1800s. Gillespie was born in the Cowpasture River Valley of Virginia in 1753. He probably learned the craft of gun making from either his Uncle Robert or from his in-laws, the Simpson family, both of whom were notable Virginia gunsmiths. As Gillespie grew up, it became clear that the two vocations he enjoyed most were hunting and gun making—and he excelled at both.

Gillespie fought against the British in the Revolutionary War. His metal working skills would save his life on March 15, 1781, at the Battle of Clapps Mill in Alamance County, North Carolina, when he carried a hand-forged tinderbox into the skirmish and a redcoat bullet deflected off it, preventing his death.

In about 1785, John sought more land and better hunting so he moved first to upstate South Carolina before permanently settling on 314 acres on the East Fork of the French Broad River, near present-day Rosman, North Carolina. It was here that he would build his gun shop and teach his three sons the art of gun building.

But it was just not the men of the clan who were involved with guns—John's wife Jane was said to have been handy with a rifle, too. She once held off a band of Cherokee marauders who attacked their homestead while John was away hunting. And one of the three Gillespie daughters—Isabel—was the best shot in the family. She tested all the early Gillespie guns for accuracy before they were sold.

"Uncle" Sammy Burchfield with his Bean rifle. *Courtesy of Great Smoky Mountains National Park Archives.*

These early Gillespie rifles were the epitome of the plain but beautifully efficient Smoky Mountain rifle. They were generally .41 to .46 in caliber, with barrels forty-five to forty-six inches long with iron hardware and a tallow hole in the stock. Soon the Gillespie guns were the favored hunting rifle on the North Carolina side of the Great Smokies. Many of the hunters of the Haywood County settlement of Cataloochee carried rifles made by John Gillespie and his family. So, too, did the white chief of the Cherokee, Colonel Will Thomas. Thomas owned a .32-caliber Gillespie hunting rifle that he later gave to a Cherokee friend. The rifle is in the Macon County, North Carolina Historical Museum today.

John Gillespie remained an avid hunter and gun maker until his death in 1822. Family lore maintains that he had a premonition of his death, but that he ignored it and went on a long hunt into the Toxaway region of the Smoky Mountains. A search party was sent looking for him after he did not return at his appointed time. They found him at his hunting camp, dead at the age of sixty-nine.

John's son Matthew moved to the Mills River, North Carolina area in 1810. He married into the Sitton family, who owned an ironworks there. With such a convenient supply of iron nearby, Matthew quickly opened his own gun shop. As a result, the creek behind his shop came to be known as Boring Branch. He and his wife Elizabeth had five sons, all of whom became gunsmiths.

Matthew Gillespie and his son Phillip would become the best known of all the Gillespie rifle makers. Their guns were a bit more elaborate than the usual Smoky Mountain rifles and often had silver, brass or gold inlays. Phillip's guns varied even more in style, some with iron hardware and some with brass. At least two of his rifles had brass patch boxes, and many of his guns had engraved barrels and ornate cross latch file work on the trigger guards. His rifles were usually in the .45-caliber range, with forty-five- to forty-seven-inch-long barrels.

Phillip Gillespie was a superb businessman who never married and had no children. Among his various business interests was a distillery where he made some of the best brandy in the Southern mountains. Phillip would supposedly accept only gold coins in payment for either his guns or brandy. Before leaving to fight for the Confederacy in the Civil War, Phillip is rumored to have taken a wagonload of brandy and gold and buried it on Forge Mountain not far from his gun shop. Phillip Gillespie and his brother Wilson both died in East Tennessee during the war. Treasure hunters still search for Gillespie's treasure today.

The last and perhaps the most talented of these Smoky Mountain rifle makers was Samuel Lafayette Click. Click was a vagabond nineteenth-century gunsmith who never owned his own shop. Instead, he preferred to move around the mountains of East Tennessee, working a month or so for room and board in local blacksmith shops, perfecting his craft and selling a few guns before moving on.

Not much is known of his past, but Click was evidently a rough sort of character. He may have learned his craft while serving time in the Tennessee State prison system. Click liked to drink and fight, and he was an exceptional hunter and marksman. Once while attending a local shooting match, the participants noted to Click that one of their friends—a drunkard known only as Joe—had passed out about one hundred yards down range from where they were gathered.

One of the group bet Click five dollars—a huge amount in 1870—that he could not shoot the toe off of Joe's boot without drawing blood. Click requested clarification on the terms. It was agreed that the bullet could not

Original Matthew Gillespie rifle. *Courtesy of Dennis Glazener.*

injure Joe, and that it had to go through both sides of his boot. Click readily accepted and fired a shot, scaring Joe so badly that he took off running. Click claimed his five dollars when they caught up with Joe and found that he was unhurt, with a bullet hole on each side of the targeted boot.

Because of his nomadic nature and wild lifestyle, not much else is known of Sam Click. But his original rifles are still admired and coveted by gun collectors and experts today. It is hard to say how much more he could have accomplished as a gun maker had he settled in one place and owned his own shop—or if he had passed his skills down to future generations, as both the Beans and Gillespies did. But then again, it was his eccentric character, as well as his skills, that helped make him a Smoky Mountain hunting legend.

By the late 1870s, lever action repeating rifles became the rage with hunters across the country, and many Smoky Mountain hunters used them too. But the muzzleloading black powder Smoky Mountain hunting rifles would continue to be used and cherished by mountain hunters until well into the early twentieth century—and no one ever used them better than the illustrious hunters of the golden age of hunting.

CHAPTER SIX

THE DAWN OF THE GOLDEN AGE

By 1840, most of the eastern band of the Cherokee tribe had been removed from their Southern mountain homelands on the infamous Trail of Tears. Only about one thousand tribal members remained in the Great Smoky Mountains, and their once vast hunting grounds were reduced from forty thousand square miles to about eighty-three square miles.

Small white settlements, farms, gristmills and hunting camps began to populate the river valleys that were once the heartland of the Cherokee nation. Yet for the most part, it is somewhat ironic that the few remaining Cherokee and their new white neighbors were remarkably similar in almost every way. They were both incredibly self-sufficient in hunting and living off the land, taking only what they needed. They lived in similar log structures, farmed the same crops, used the same weapons to hunt, dressed much the same way and they often worshiped the same Christian God. Both hunting cultures possessed a fierce sense of independence, and they adhered to a strict code of honor that tolerated no insults—real or imagined. And while many preferred to be left alone, they were loyal to a fault to family and friends.

Most of the time these folks recognized their commonalities, respected each other and often were friends. In many ways this peaceful coexistence is similar—though in reverse—to earlier times when the first white traders and hunters lived happily as a minority among the mountain Cherokee. Like these earlier times, wild game was still plentiful in the Great Smoky Mountains.

For these reasons, as well as because of the isolated nature of the Great Smokies, a new golden age era of hunting began in the Southern mountains. This era would encompass more than a century, from about 1840 to 1945, and it would produce some of the most remarkable hunters the world has ever seen. Four of the best of these early nimrods—Fredrick Messer, Israel Medford, Montraville Plott and George Palmer—earned their hunting spurs in Haywood County, North Carolina.

Frederick "Uncle Fed" Messer

While it is debatable if he was the best of the old-time hunters, not many can argue that Fredrick Messer lived to be the oldest. Messer, who was better known as Uncle Fed, was born in 1792 in Lincoln County, North Carolina. When he was four years old, his family moved to Dutch Cove in Haywood County near present-day Canton, North Carolina. But the land was not wild enough for the Messer clan, who soon moved to better hunting grounds in western Haywood County on Panther Creek, a tributary of the Pigeon River.

As he grew into manhood, Uncle Fed was easily identifiable due to his large stature and because he almost always wore his shirt unbuttoned and open to the waist. He once said that he had only buttoned his shirt twice in his lifetime—once when he got married in 1828 and another time in the winter of 1840, when it was said to be so cold that if you threw out a bucket of water it would be frozen before it hit the ground.

Messer had a reputation for being one of the finest hunters and best shots in a county well-known for them. He put these skills and his long legs to good use, tramping many miles throughout the Great Smokies harvesting all sorts of game—often barefoot. He hiked the twenty-two miles from his homestead to the county seat in Waynesville twice a year for supplies, allowing two days to make the round trip. It took him three days to make the same trip when he was 109 years old—and he then complained that old age was catching up with him.

Though he could not read or write, Uncle Fed took his civic responsibilities seriously. He remembered the first time he ever voted for two reasons— one was the candidate that he voted for, James Madison, and the other was because of a man he had to whip who had tried to prevent him from voting.

Perhaps Messer's most exciting hunt was the time he killed a "panther" using only the butt of his flintlock rifle. Uncle Fed told Haywood County historian Clark Medford that one of his hunting dogs had "got after a panther and got into a fight with it." He could not get off a shot without risking his dog, so Uncle Fed waded into the fray and turned the butt of his gun on the big cat, killing it instantly. His dog, though still alive, was badly

Searching the Tree Tops, pencil
drawing by David Wright.

wounded. Fed took the hound home and cooked the panther for the dog to eat. According to Uncle Fed, "Hit lasted my dawg until he got well."

Messer was strong and healthy most of his life and he always insisted on testing himself. When he was 100 years old, he walked into town and told a crowd at the courthouse that he could do something none of them could do. He then proceeded to dance a spirited jig around the square. But that wasn't enough. To celebrate his 107th birthday, he swam back and forth across the Pigeon River just to prove that he could.

Uncle Fed outlived his wife and nine children and he died in February 1907, just shy of his 115th birthday. He still hunted regularly until shortly before his death. A few days before he died, Uncle Fed told Clark Medford that he certainly hoped there was hunting allowed in heaven. The old hunter's life had stretched across parts or all of three centuries, beginning in the time of our first President George Washington and ending during the administration of our twenty-sixth president, Teddy Roosevelt.

Israel "Wid" Medford

Another early golden age hunting legend was Israel "Wid" Medford. Wid, born in 1818, was known as the "master bear hunter of the Balsams." He lived on a huge farm with his wife and their fourteen children at the base of Lickstone Mountain, about five miles south of Waynesville. Wid would help his family plant and harvest their crops in the spring and fall, but he otherwise devoted his time entirely to hunting for his own family or as a paid guide.

Today, master gunsmith and artist Earl Lanning and his wife Bonnie live near the site of the Medford homeplace. Mrs. Lanning is Wid Medford's great-great-granddaughter, and two paintings of Wid hang in their home. Both are great paintings, but one of them truly captures the essence of a mountain nimrod. Wid is shown seated on a stump in full hunting attire— fur cap, hunting shirt, breeches and sturdy brogans—with a look of sheer bliss on his finely chiseled face. A powder horn and a big hunting knife are attached to the strap of the shot bag hanging from his shoulder. His trusty flintlock rifle lies across his knee and he is surrounded by a fine pack of mountain cur hunting dogs.

Earl Lanning shared this story with me about Medford: It had been a hard winter, the bears were in hibernation and game was strangely scarce. It was one of those times when nothing was stirring in the woods, not even chipmunks, and even a hunter as highly skilled as Wid Medford was hard pressed to "make meat." Nevertheless, Wid left his home to hunt in the rugged Caney Fork area of nearby Jackson County, North Carolina. Confident in both his survival skills and his abilities to find *something* to hunt or eat, Wid, as usual, traveled light with few provisions.

After three days he had found no game sign, and he had eaten little himself. He doggedly pressed on, determined not to return home empty-handed. Two more days passed and, weakened from hunger, he decided to return home. However, his directional capabilities were impaired due to his weary condition, and he became hopelessly lost. He wandered aimlessly for another day or two until he finally crossed a ridge and saw a woman hanging out laundry at a cabin far below. Wid thought he was hallucinating. He gathered his last bit of strength to shout, "Hello down thar! Who lives down thar?" To which the lady replied "You, you old fool, this is YOUR house!"

Even in this frail state his human compass had remained accurate, though his body was so exhausted that he was unable to recognize his own home and family. It was one of the few times that the old woodsman failed to bring home meat and probably the only time he was ever lost. While Wid did not match Uncle Fed Messer in lifespan longevity, he more than made up for that in enthusiasm—especially his love for hunting with dogs and the thrill of the chase.

Plumb Wore Down, pencil drawing
by David Wright.

Authors Wilbur Zeigler and Ben Grosscup first met Medford in 1883 in his hunting camp about eight miles south of Waynesville, North Carolina. Medford was sixty-five years old then, but he was still recognized as a robust man who could run men half his age into the ground. In their 1883 book *The Heart of the Alleghenies or Western North Carolina*, the writers offer this description of the old hunter: "He is a singular character and a good representative of an old class of mountaineers, who reared in the wilderness, still spend most of their time hunting and fishing."

They go on to describe him physically as being bow-legged and having "long grey hair, keen blue eyes, a clear, ruddy, hatchet shaped face, bare but for a red mustache." The authors also felt that his animated storytelling skills nearly matched his capabilities as a master mountain hunter. Wid maintained that no man alive knew the Smoky Mountains better than he did: "What I don't know about these mountains hain't of any profit to man or devil. Why, I've fit bars from the Dark Ridge country to the headwaters of the French Broad. I've brogued it through every briar patch and laurel thicket from here to the South Caroliny and Georgy lines."

Medford then regaled the writers with a tale of a bear hunt he was once on near Scotts Creek in neighboring Jackson County. He and some friends and their dogs had run a bear for almost twenty-four hours when the bruin turned and charged them. Wid estimated the bear to be close to five hundred pounds, and being worn out himself he wanted to finally end this hunt—or else lose his life.

Wid brought his flintlock rifle to his shoulder—he still preferred them over more modern guns—and shot the charging bear, to no avail. He tells the rest of the story in his own unique manner:

> *The brute never stopped, but I knowed I'd hit him, for I had a dead sight on his head; and like blockade whiskey, a ball outa that black bore always goes to the spot. I dropped my gun and pulled my knife. On he come. He didn't pay no more attention to me than if I had been a rock. I drew back a step and as he brashed by me, I bent over him, grabbin' the hair of his neck with one hand, and I stabbed him deep in the side with the knife in the other. That's all I knowed for hours.*

When asked if he had fainted, Wid replied: "Fainted? You ass! You don't reckon I faint do you? Women faint. I fell dead! You see, all the blood in me jumped over my heart into my head, and of course hit finished me for a time. But the boys and dogs come on me a second after. Bill Allen cut my veins, and in a short time I come around, but I was sick for a week."

Someone then questioned him as to what had happened to the big bear: "Hit lay dead by the branch below, stabbed clean through the heart."

On another bear hunt, Medford faced another charging bear and reached for his knife but found that it was gone. Wid recalled, "I memorize one time that I war in a tight box. Hit war down on the Pigeon where the laurel is too thick fer a covey of partridges to riz from. Thar war one straight trail and I war in it. My gun war empty."

As he heard the bear charging toward him, hotly pursued by his pack of dogs, Wid had nowhere to go and no time to reload his gun. He continued:

> *I never had no objections ter meetin' a varmint in a squar stand up fight— his nails agin my knife, ye know; so without thinkin' on gittin' outer the way, I retched fer my sticker. The tarnal thing war gone and thar me without a weapon big enough to skin a boomer. I run along lookin' at the laurel on both sides, but thar warn't a place in it fer a man ter get even one leg in. Ticklish? You're sound thar! I didn't know what the devil to do. Well, I dropped on my elbows and knees square across the narrow path.*

Medford resigned himself to his pending doom as the bear rumbled toward him. He looked over his shoulder as it neared him:

Har hit come, a big monster brute with a loose tongue hangin' out and red eyes. He war trottin' like a stage hoss. He never stopped even to sniff me, but puttin' his paws on my back as tho' I war a log, he jist leaped over me and he war out of sight in a jerk. The dogs were close on his heels, a' snappin' away, and every one of them jumped over me and raced along without ever stoppin' to lick thar masters hand!

Though Wid enjoyed hunting all types of game, it was bear hunting that he clearly enjoyed the most. And not just any type of bear hunting either—for Wid Medford, nothing could beat hunting bear with dogs. He elaborated, "Traps is good fer them that hunts rabbits, and rabbit hunting is good fer boys. But fer me, give me my old flintlock shooting iron and let a keen pack of lean hounds be hoppin' ahead. And of all sports, the master sport is following their music over the mountains, and winding up with a bullet or sticker in a varminous old bear!"

When asked if he loved bear hunting, Wid simply exclaimed *"Good Law!"* He then described what he would do if he could live his life over again: "I'd get me a neat woman and go to the wildest country in creation and

No Stronger Bond, painting by David Wright.

hunt from the day I was big enough to tote a rifle gun, until old age and roomaticks fastened in on me!"

That is exactly what the "master hunter of the Balsams" did—and he never had to leave his beloved Smoky Mountains to do it. Wid Medford died in 1905, at the age of eighty-seven, in Haywood County, the place of his birth. No one knows for sure how many bears he killed in his long lifetime of hunting, but it is unlikely that anyone ever enjoyed hunting any more than he did.

Montraville "Mont" Plott

A Haywood County bear hunter who *did* keep a tally of his bear kills was Montraville "Mont" Plott. It is doubtful that there is another family of Smoky Mountain bear hunters that can match the Plott family in either its hunting longevity or its bear hunting skills. But it is certain that no one can surpass their prized hunting dogs—known today as the Plott bear hound.

By the time of his birth in 1850, Montraville Plott's family had been bear hunting with their Plott hounds in America for almost a century. Mont's great-grandfather Johannes (George) Plott first came to this country with five of the family dogs in 1750, and it was his son, Henry (Mont's grandpa), who first brought the dogs to the Great Smokies in about 1800. Henry and his wife Lydia had eleven children, eight of them boys, and nearly all of the lads became renowned hunters and dog breeders.

One of these eight sons was John T. Plott. John was not as well-known as his more famous brothers, Amos, David and Enos, but he was nonetheless recognized as a fine hunter and dog man in his own right. And it was John's son—Montraville "Mont" Plott—who truly brought fame to the Plott clan.

Mont grew up hunting on the almost two thousand acres that his grandfather Henry had claimed for the family in 1800. This area, as well as the surrounding mountain range, is now known respectively as Plott Valley and the Plott Balsams. Both are near present-day Waynesville, North Carolina, only a few miles from the Wid Medford place. Like Wid, Mont could not have picked a better place to hone his hunting and dog breeding skills. Wild game was abundant, and he did not have to range too far from his farm with his dogs to find it.

Plott was known to be a serious hunter with no time for small talk. If there was an outlaw bear that no one else could kill, it was Mont Plott who usually got the call. The nearby community of Mount Sterling was considered by many to be not only a remote place, but also an area well-known for being populated by rough folks, some of whom hid out there from the law. The citizens of Mount Sterling liked to be left alone. They disliked any sort of interference by anyone—even their mountain neighbors.

But in the late 1880s, a huge rogue bear plagued the area, killing livestock and attacking local farms. Even the hardy hunters of Mount Sterling were no match for this bruin, which killed just for enjoyment and often left the carcasses of its victims uneaten. A call was sent out for Mont Plott and his Plott dogs to come and see what they could do.

Legend has it that Mont arrived in Mount Sterling a day or two later. He was quite a dashing figure astride his favorite black stallion, his bear pistol holstered on his McClellan saddle, with four or five of his top bear dogs leading the way and a pack horse bringing up the rear. Mont softly asked the location of the latest bear attack. He then rode off in that direction without saying another word. About a day later, Mont rode back to the settlement with the dead bear tied to his pack horse. His work was done. He left quietly for home.

During the course of his hunting career, Mont Plott killed 211 bears—all of them with that single-shot muzzleloading black powder pistol. His hunting skills were so finely honed and his fierce dogs were so well trained that he could approach a bear at close range and almost always make the kill with a single shot.

As he grew older, Mont was determined to continue hunting, but he found himself often physically unable to closely follow his dogs. He adapted by having his hunting partners handle some of his start dogs as they struck a trail, while he would position himself strategically in nearby mountain gaps that he anticipated the bear would be driven to.

In bear hunting terms this is known as a "stander." In other words, the hunters with the strike dogs are "drivers" who hit a bear trail and run the bear toward the stander, who either makes the kill himself or releases more bear dogs to "pack" the trail. Sometimes, though, the drivers will tree or bay the bear first and make the kill themselves.

In his later years, Mont hunted often as a stander. Once he was accompanied by inexperienced hunters, one of whom asked Mont if he could shoot the bear. Mont agreed that he could, but warned him that under no circumstances was he to let the bear get by without making the kill. Mont then left the rookie hunter to return to his own stand that was close by.

Things went exactly as planned. Mont listened carefully as he heard the dogs chase the bear right by the greenhorn hunter—but to his chagrin he heard no gunfire as the bear and hounds crossed the gap and charged into the valley below. Mont hurriedly approached the man and angrily asked

Muzzleloading, single-shot, black powder pistol used by Montraville Plott to kill 211 bears. *Plott family collection.*

him why he had not taken the shot. Plott then noticed a rank aroma and he realized that the hunter had been so scared that he had defecated on himself. "Did you shit your pants?" he asked. "Yes," the terrified hunter replied, "but not enough to notice!" Mont obviously could. He stalked angrily away, trying hard not to laugh.

For all his many hunting accolades, Mont Plott is probably best known for two things: his "tow sack network" of distributing Plott hounds and his famous hunting sons—particularly John and Vaughn "Von" Plott—who themselves became modern-day Smoky Mountain hunting legends. Mont's reputation as a hunter and dog breeder was such that families across the mountains would come annually to the Plott farm to get pups from him. By spreading his dogs across the mountains to elite hunters and by continuing to refine the breed himself, Mont ensured that the hunting legacy of his ancestral dogs would be correctly perpetuated. And it was. Thanks to Mont Plott, and later his more famous sons, John and Von, the Plott bear hound is today generally recognized as the premier big game hunting dog in the world.

Montraville Plott, age seventy, circa 1920, with Plott pup. *Plott family collection.*

"Turkey" George Palmer

The magnificent high mountain valley of Cataloochee is tucked away in the northwest corner of Haywood County, North Carolina, and it is bordered by the Qualla Boundary of the Cherokee and the state of Tennessee. The remote valley's name is derived from the Cherokee word *Gadalutsi*, which is said to mean "standing in a row." This alludes to either the row after row of mountain peaks or the many fir trees that surround the valley.

Today the valley is best known as an elk habitat in the Great Smoky Mountain National Park. But years ago, Cataloochee was the home of some of the best hunters in the Great Smoky Mountains. Some of the earliest settlers in Cataloochee were the Palmer family. One of their sons, George, would become arguably the most famous hunter in the history of the valley.

George Palmer was born in Cataloochee in 1857. As a boy he greatly enjoyed hunting, and he earned the nickname of "Turkey George" when he was about eleven years old. It seems that the lad had developed a great talent for building turkey traps or pens. These brush-covered traps were built on a sloping hill, and they were about ten feet wide and ten feet long. A tunnel was dug under the trap and baited to lead the gobblers into it. Once inside, the turkey was usually unable to get back out. And even if they tried, hunters were on guard to cover their escape tunnel.

George was better than most in building these pens, but he exceeded even his own expectations when he returned one day to find seven turkeys in his trap. Even though he was armed with his flintlock rifle, the young hunter did not feel it would be "sporting" to shoot the turkeys from the outside of the pen. So he decided to just crawl into the pen with them and wring their necks. That was a big mistake. The seven big turkeys in close quarters nearly beat the unarmed boy senseless. Though battered, he somehow managed to eventually kill them all. He tied the feet of the dead birds together and threw three over his left shoulder, four over his right and returned home. From that day forward he was known as "Turkey" George Palmer.)

Turkey George wasn't a big man. He stood only about five feet, eight inches tall, and he weighed in at about 140 sinewy pounds. But he was an exceptional bear hunter, though he harvested most of them by trapping. His favorite trapping lands were on Big Butt Mountain between Beech Creek and Pretty Hollow Creek. Turkey George killed 106 bears in his sporting career and his wife always knew when he was bringing bear meat home. Robert Palmer, the son of Turkey George, recalled to Mark Hannah, "My mother always could tell before my father got to the house whether he had got a bear. When my father got to Butt Mountain—that was just off above the homeplace between here and Pretty Hollow Creek—he would let out a powerful yell. When he done that, my mother knew to get the water boiling. She knew he had a bear and would fetch it along directly."

Turkey George had two bear trapping seasons—in the fall when they were their heaviest and in the spring after they came out of hibernation. He trapped his biggest bear when he was sixty-two years old in March 1919. A huge bruin had killed several of his hogs, so Turkey George tracked the bear and eventually trapped and killed it. The rogue bear weighed almost 530 pounds.

Like many old-time hunters, Turkey George found ways to make money while doing what he loved. Any bear meat not used by his family was canned and sold for $1.50 per jar. He also hunted and sold ginseng. He took advantage of the bounty on wolves that plagued the valley and killed many of those, too. Palmer said that the wolves were too smart to be trapped, so he often had to resort to poisoning them with mutton laced with strychnine.

Palmer was not only a great trapper, but he was a fine marksman as well. His son Robert recalled that George often hunted squirrels and that he would

"Turkey" George Palmer in 1935.
Courtesy of Great Smoky Mountains National Park Archives.

shoot their heads off with his muzzleloading rifle. He added that he had seen his father make six straight head shots on the boomers, and that he "barked" three more. Barking is a term used to describe shooting the limb or bark out from under the squirrel, stunning it and causing it to fall to the ground. By doing this, the hunter does not damage the meat with the lead shot or ball.

Though the earlier hunters in the valley had thinned out the local deer population—almost to extinction by 1860—Turkey George Palmer still managed to kill twenty deer in his lifetime. But it was the one that got away from him that his brother Will Palmer would always remember. Will recalled that he and his brother were deer hunting when a big buck charged them. It is hard to say who was surprised the most—the Palmer brothers or the deer. The big buck jumped over Turkey George's head, knocking him down with its hindquarters as it ran away. Will said that was "the only time Turkey George acknowledged defeat at the heels of a deer."

The Squirrel Hunter, pencil drawing
by David Wright.

For all his skills as a hunter, Turkey George was equally as well-known
for his quick wit and charming sense of humor. He once told a friend who
was suffering from a severe hangover, "Your eyes look like a red fox's ass in
a pokeberry patch." Another time he spun a tall tale of the hunt where he
found six turkeys perched on a limb. Palmer was armed only with his single-
shot rifle and he was faced with the dilemma of how to kill them all with one
bullet. After pondering over it a moment, Turkey George fired one shot and
split the limb in two, thus capturing the claws of the turkeys in its grasp. He
then wrung their necks one by one and took his bounty home.

As he grew older, Turkey George continued to hunt as often as he was
able, and he kept pet raccoons to amuse the visitors who often came to hear
his great hunting stories. Shortly before his death, he instructed his family
to make sure that his coffin was specially constructed of steel because he
did not want the local bear population to take their revenge on his dead
body. According to his daughter, Flora Palmer, the family honored his wishes
and buried the old hunter in a steel coffin when he died in 1944 at the age
of eighty-seven. Though his homeland is now owned by the National Park
Service, Turkey George Palmer will forever be remembered as one of the
greatest hunters in the valley of Cataloochee.

CHAPTER SEVEN

TENNESSEE RIDGE RUNNERS

Just over the mountain on the Tennessee side of the Great Smokies lived another group of amazing golden age hunters. In a mountain range well-known for its fabled figures, a good argument can be made that none surpass those who resided and hunted in these isolated coves, peaks and valleys.

In the early 1900s, writer Robert Lindsay Mason often hunted with these Tennessee ridge runners while compiling information for his 1927 book *The Lure of the Great Smokies*. Like his contemporary Horace Kephart, Mason had no problem in gaining acceptance from these mountaineers who evidently appreciated his skill and stamina. But unlike many writers, before and since, Mason clearly respected and admired the subjects of his work and he did not stoop to use the typical "ignorant hillbilly" stereotypes in describing them.

Mason mentioned many great hunters in his book, men such as Cades Cove residents Uncle Sammy Burchfield and George Powell—who both owned rifles made by the Bean family—and he told of their many skills. But Mason focused mainly on the hunters who we will profile in this chapter. Unless otherwise noted, all quotes in this chapter came from Mason's book, which is now unfortunately out of print.

William "Black Bill" Walker

In an era when even the average hunter would be extraordinary by our standards, William "Black Bill" Walker stands out as a man of almost mythical proportions. There are many reasons for this. His multiple talents would make him worthy of mention in any historical study of the region. After all, he was the founding member of his own settlement, he owned an entire valley and he was a capable farmer, cattleman, miller, arborist and beekeeper, as well as an exceptional hunter and storyteller. But so were many others.

It was his fierce protection of his valley from lumber barons, his unconventional lifestyle and his flamboyant personality, combined with an almost insatiable lust for the wilderness and women that truly made Black Bill Walker legendary. The fact that Walker was readily accepted, even admired, by many of his more stoic and conventional neighbors only adds to his mystique. Perhaps they appreciated that he was no hypocrite, and that he made no apologies for how he lived. There is nothing that mountain folks respect more than honesty, and Black Bill Walker *was* honest. He lived his life openly for all to see. This is probably why respected men of the cloth such as Preacher John Stinnett called Walker a friend and hunting partner. Whether you agree with him or not, you have to respect him. This is his story.

William Walker was born in 1838 in Tuckaleechee Cove near present-day Townsend, Tennessee. He often referred to himself as "the old trapper from the Tuckaleechee." His father was a frontier Presbyterian preacher and his mother, a Scot, was from the McGill clan. Growing up the son of one of the earliest settlers in the Smokies, William early on mastered the multipurpose talents needed for survival in those remote backwoods. Farming, building gristmills, animal husbandry—Black Bill could do it all, but hunting was his true passion. Or as he best described it to Robert Mason, "I always was somewhat of a fool about the woods. I live in them just because I love 'em. When I was young, they wasn't nothing about the mountains that I didn't want to learn and they wasn't no risky thing that I didn't want to do."

He sometimes sought the advice of his Indian neighbors to learn the Cherokee tricks of woodcraft. He and a friend, Devil Sam Walker, once visited some Cherokee hunters in Yellow Hill on the Qualla Boundary. Their hosts invited the boys to spend the night with them. Black Bill later said that as he and Sam were drifting off to sleep, the older hunters began to argue angrily in their native tongue. The lads spoke no Cherokee, but they were convinced that the Indians were debating as to how they should kill the boys and who would get their scalps.

The youngsters quietly escaped from the house, but they later learned that the joke was on them. It turned out that the men were deacons in a Cherokee Baptist church and they were arguing about a member who was to be "churched," or excommunicated. However, Black Bill had many other opportunities to learn from the Cherokee and the lessons served him well the remainder of his life.

As he grew into manhood, Walker was tagged with two nicknames—"Big Bill" for his physique and "Black Bill" for his dark features. He packed 190 pounds of muscle on his six-foot, two-inch frame, and he often said that he was "mostly muscle and the rest fool!" With his powerful build and long, coal black hair and beard, combined with his piercing ebony eyes and dark skin, Black Bill Walker was a striking figure.

Nineteen-year-old Nancy Caylor surely thought so. Black Bill claimed her as his wife when he was twenty-one years old. In 1859, they set out to make a place of their own and they found it in the beautiful Tennessee valley now known as Tremont. There the Walkers claimed two thousand acres of land and started a community then known as Walker's Valley. Their cabin was located on the middle prong of the Little River at the foot of the Great Smoky range. Nancy soon had the first of their seven children, as Bill cleared land, planted crops and built gristmills. But no matter how hard he worked, Black Bill always made time to hunt—partly because his family needed it as a food source, but also because it was his first love.

Black Bill built his own rifle especially for bear hunting. He named it "Old Death." The huge bore rifle shot a two-ounce ball that could knock down the biggest bruin. The monster gun was as long as its owner and weighed more than twenty pounds. Only a man of Black Bill's strength and stature could handle a gun this big. It served him well—most of the time.

When he was twenty-three years old in 1861, he embarked on a hunt that he would never forget. The Civil War was in full swing as Union General James Longstreet lay siege to nearby Knoxville, Tennessee. Black Bill could hear cannon fire in the distance as he left alone on this record hunt.

Arriving in the Meigs Mountain area, Walker was shocked to find seven or eight full-grown bears frolicking in the leaves searching for chestnuts. Black Bill recalled, "Well! Right then I got nervous. I thought that I'd come to a bear convention!" He dropped to one knee and attempted a shot, but his flintlock would not spark. Walker quickly knapped the flint and fired again, this time hitting a bear, but not killing it.

Black Bill said that it was then that he was struck by the "the bear augue." He was nervous and shaking so badly that he could barely reload his rifle. But he did, and when he looked up again the bear was gone. Bill followed the bloody trail, found the animal and shot it a second time—but the rifle misfired, this time due to bad priming powder. However, the rifle did go off, albeit late, causing Bill to only wing the bruin. Black Bill carefully reloaded and fired another shot. This time he was sure that the bear was dead. He reloaded a third time and cautiously approached the beast. He kneeled beside the bear and prodded it with his rifle. To his dismay, the jaws and teeth of the bear snapped shut on his gun like a steel trap. He managed to wrench the rifle away and finally shot the bear dead.

Black Bill Walker and his wife, the former Nancy Caylor, about 1910. *Courtesy of Great Smoky Mountains National Park Archives.*

Walker field dressed the bear and headed back home, killing a second bear on the way. He was down to his last powder charge when he ran into yet another bear and killed it. He cached the meat and his provisions in a cave and rushed back to the cabin of his friends, Sammy and Danny Burchfield. Black Bill staggered out of breath into the door, as his friends asked what was wrong. Walker replied, "I got three bears and I seen twenty more!" The next day Black Bill and five of his friends killed six more bears, four in only ten minutes, an all-time record for the group.

Black Bill's love for the hunt was surpassed only by his daring. His friend Jeff Wear once bayed a bear. He offered Bill the bear hide if he would go into a cave and get it. On his first attempt, Walker made a spear and crawled in the bear den. But the sow bear shattered the spear and sent him scurrying out. He returned for a second try, this time with his rifle, and crawled closer to the bruin. But she knocked the gun from his hands, partially splintering the stock. Bill managed to retrieve the gun and was

Black Bill Walker
and his Smoky
Mountain rifle,
"Old Death," about
1910. *Courtesy of
Great Smoky Mountains
National Park Archives.*

able to get off a point blank shot, instantly killing the bear. He got his hide and kept the cubs for pets.

Recalling that dangerous stunt, Black Bill later said, "I was sure risky in them days. I was just a plain fool in many respects." After thinking a moment he added, "Fool? I was just plain RISKY!"

Like many mountaineers, Black Bill was a bit superstitious and he placed a great deal of stock in dreams. He said that once he was troubled nightly by the same dream. In it, a witch turned him into a horse and rode him deep into the mountains to a magic square dance held in a cave. After dancing all night, the witch would ride him back home at daybreak and then turn him back to human form. Black Bill would awake at dawn, totally exhausted, his restful sleep ruined.

Believing the dream was a sign, Walker spent his days searching for the enchanted cave, but he never could find it. He then decided that the next time he had the dream he would bite the bark on the tree that the witch tied him to and mark the ground by pawing it with his hooves. To further ensure that he could locate the cave, he decided to leave horse droppings too.

That night he had the same dream again. As usual, he was changed to a horse, ridden to exhaustion and tethered at the cave. Black Bill continued, "Thar I was, a pony, standing by the cave hitched. The music started and she lit and went in. I begun to gnaw the bush and paw the log something tremendous; and the droppings too. I pawed thunder out of that log, but somebody started yelling, Will! Will! What on earth are ye trying to do, kill me?"

Walker said it was then that he woke up to the screams of his wife as he pawed her out of the bed while trying to gnaw on the headboards. Worse of all, he had left some human "horse droppings" of his own in the bed to mark his location. Black Bill said that it was then that he quit believing in witches.

As he grew older, Black Bill Walker literally and figuratively became the patriarch of Walker Valley. In addition to the seven children that he fathered with his wife Nancy, Black Bill also had numerous other children with many common-law wives. Some reports indicate that there were no more than twenty-nine, while others maintain that Walker fathered as many as forty-two children out of wedlock. Regardless of the actual number, there were no doubt a *lot* of them. Perhaps more importantly, it is interesting to note how he rationalized doing this and how he did it openly with no apparent problems.

There has been speculation that Black Bill was a Mormon and that he justified his behavior as a religious right. That is doubtful considering his

Jim Moore and his hunting dog Huldagard. Jim was the son of Black Bill Walker and Mary Anne Moore. *Courtesy of Great Smoky Mountains National Park Archives.*

background and the fact that few, if any, Mormons were in the area then. Moreover, he told Mason that he had been "churched" or thrown out of the local Presbyterian congregation as a young man, and he implied that he had never went back to that church or any other. More than likely it was simply the way that Black Bill Walker had chosen to live as a freeborn mountaineer who answered to no one.

But an even bigger question is how he managed to openly live this lifestyle and get by with it. After all, the fact that Black Bill was able to remain married for more than thirty years, and was never shot by his wife, his common-law wives or any of their relatives is probably more impressive than any of his other accolades. The fact that he had a well-earned reputation as a man not to be trifled with and that he was a crack shot certainly didn't hurt. But even that wouldn't have allowed him to die a natural death back in those days. If he had been some shady figure, regardless of how formidable, someone would have eventually bushwhacked him.

I believe that he survived because he was honest about himself and he was accountable for his actions. By all accounts he was a generous man and he took care of all his children. He spearheaded the efforts to see that a school was started in the valley. One of his children, whom Walker had sent to college, came back and taught there. His honesty and accountability, combined with his generous and gregarious personality, all factored into making Bill Walker a well-liked and respected man.

Black Bill Walker led a full and long life. He attributed his health and longevity to this simple philosophy: "I wouldn't a got old so quick if the wild game had kept up but when that begun to get scarce I begun to fall off. That's what keeps a man young and makes him strong; hit's wild game and the likes of it, without coffee, backer [tobacco] and bad liquor."

The old hunter reflected a moment and continued: "I'm better off than some of the fellers that lives down in the coves nigh town. I live betwixt two fogs up here. The upper fog lies high on the mountain tops and it don't shut me out from the Almighty; but the lower fog shuts me out from the disputes preachers is having about which way is right; this and the other. And after all, I may be better off than what I think!"

As the twentieth century began, lumber barons came into the mountains, buying land for nearly nothing and clear cutting it. They quickly targeted the original hardwoods of Walker Valley, but Walker would have no part of it. While many around him sold out, he held out as long as he could until shortly before his death, at the age of eighty-one in 1919.

William "Black Bill" Walker lived a remarkable life. Regardless of anyone's opinion regarding his lifestyle, Walker was truly a Smoky Mountain hunting legend of epic proportions. He will be remembered forever by many generations to come—and understandably so, as so many of them are probably related to him!

The Stinnett Brothers

Bill, Henry and John Stinnett were all well-known throughout the Smokies as being crack shots and expert hunters. Like most golden age hunters, the Stinnetts still used the old-time Smoky Mountain rifles, and in the case of John, it was a rifle that he had made himself.

Henry Stinnett was the oldest of the brothers and, like the others, he greatly enjoyed bear hunting. Unlike many of their counterparts on the North Carolina side of the Smokies, most of the Tennessee hunters did not use dogs. They instead preferred to "still hunt," which means they either scouted for bear sign and tracked the bear or else they hid quietly where bears were known to reside. Henry once got close enough to a bear that he was able to stick his rifle into its ribs and shoot it dead. He said the massive bruin weighed well over four hundred pounds.

Mason doesn't relate much about the youngest Stinnett brother, Bill, who lived near Spruce Flats, except to note that Bill Stinnett was well respected as a trapper and a guide. However, it was John Stinnett, better known as

Preacher John, in whom Mason seemed the most interested. Like his father before him, Preacher John Stinnett was a "hard-shell" primitive Baptist minister. As a young man, John spent every free moment he had hunting. But when he was called to the ministry he cut back on it quite a bit, or as he described it, "I don't hunt as much as I used to, because the Lord wanted me fer to be a hunter and fisher o' men. I was an expert, you might say at both huntin' and fishin', but now my ammunition is the powder of the word and the bullet of faith, and if I shoot straight as I used to, I might bring down a game a heap sight more valuable maybe!"

But even with his religious obligations, Preacher John remained a fearsome hunter and a reliable hunting partner. Stinnett lived with his family in a cabin in Little Greenbrier Cove, about ten miles north of his friend Black Bill Walker. Mason described Stinnett as a modest and friendly fellow who was the sort of old-time preacher who "could shoot as well as he can pray." Preacher John was a tall man with a lean, muscular frame. He had a bushy gray mustache and his keen gray eyes always sparkled with good humor.

Black Bill Walker recalled his friend as being a fine hunter with great stamina, but noted that he had an unusual style of running: "John was a comical hunter when he'd get excited. He always run like a stiff legged jay bird and he'd fire and fall back, using regular military tactics."

According to no less an expert than Walker, it was Preacher John who killed the biggest bear ever seen in the Great Smoky Mountains. Walker, Preacher John and his brother Henry were hunting a stock killing bear in the Laurel Gap area when a big bear charged them out of the fog. Preacher John shot the bruin dead and the party cautiously approached the massive beast to examine it. It was an old bear, scarred from past battles and with well-worn tusks. The green hide of the bruin alone weighed almost one hundred pounds, and its length from root of tail to base of ears measured nine feet. The hunters all agreed that the bear weighed well over six hundred pounds. It was indeed a grizzly sized beast and it was killed by Preacher John Stinnett with a flintlock rifle made by his own talented hands. Stinnett later said that he was paid $4.50 for the huge bear hide.

Like most golden age hunters, Stinnett adhered to a strict code of conduct in the woods. He would never shoot a doe or a fawn or kill a bear cub, and like the early Cherokee, he never took more game than he needed. He said, "We didn't have no game laws in our time and we didn't need them. We did have some principle, though, and we didn't shoot any more than we could eat or give to desirin' neighbors."

Preacher John Stinnett was a supremely talented man—hunter, farmer, preacher, carpenter and gun maker. But he was also an insightful and

Preacher John Stinnett at his home in Little Greenbrier Cove. *Courtesy of Great Smoky Mountains National Park Archives.*

philosophical sort of fellow. One of his sons returned from combat in World War I a hollow shell of his former self. Stinnett told Mason with his voice breaking:

> *Thar's my boy, he come back all buggered up. Ain't worth much now. He got the German poison gas and it appears like he ain't the same. War is an awful thing and it oughtent to be. If them fellers hate each other, let them settle their own differences, we ain't fighting nobody's quarrel in foreign countries! But they ought ter remember that the Book says that them that takes the sword must perish by it.*

Stinnett also offered his theory to Mason that wars are started by kings and politicians to make money and to kill off the poor people whom they did not want to be bothered with. He also suggested that all future wars be fought with flintlocks to prevent so many casualties.

Preacher John Stinnett was a true hunting legend of the Great Smoky Mountains. But he was much more than that. He was a man who was wise well beyond any sort of formal education and a man whose words still ring true today.

Levi Trentham and Ben Parton

Many golden age hunters could brag that they had killed bears or boars with a knife in hand to paw combat. But only Levi Trentham could lay claim to killing a bear while armed only with a pine knot!

Levi was a short but strongly built man who lived and hunted in the Sugarlands area of East Tennessee. Even in an era when most men wore beards, Levi was easily distinguished by his unique whiskers. His vast beard covered the bulk of his upper torso, and it stretched almost to his waist. With his distinctive facial hair, large ears, quick smile and mischievous nature, Levi Trentham was easy to spot and fun to be around.

While he may not have been as well-known as the Stinnett brothers or Black Bill Walker, Levi was no less a hunter. In the late 1800s, he set a trap for a bear that had been killing his livestock. While unarmed in the area checking on his pigs, he found that the bear was indeed in the trap, but just barely, and that it was feisty and ready to fight for its life.

Levi told Robert Mason what happened next:

> *Thar he was a snarlin' and a snappin' and layin' back his tushes at me. I didn't have no gun, but the thoughts of them pigs I was losin' jest went all over me and I flew into a temper. Thar was a heavy pine knot a layin' thar and before I thought I had snatched hit up and I was belaborin' that bear as he was boxin' with me tryin' to slap that weapon outer my hand. We fit up an down for a spell. After a while I give him a crack that seemed to daze him and seein' my chance I run in and let him have a good one on the ear and down he went, I had finished him. The hook of that trap was cotched on a little root no bigger than my finger and if he'd made a lunge I wouldn't a been here to tell this tale.*

In fairness to the bear, it must again be noted that it *was* caught in a bear trap. This was not the case, however, when Levi and his friend Ben Parton found a bear den filled with almost twenty bears and crawled into it. We

Levi Trentham at Elkmont. *Courtesy of Great Smoky Mountains National Park Archives.*

have so few firsthand accounts of golden age hunters today that it is best to let Ben tell the story in his own words:

Levi and me was out amblin' about one heavy snow and studying tracks and we seen whar b'ars was comin' out of a cave gittin' water. Ye didn't know bars drunk winter all winter, did ye? Ye thought they jest holed up some whar and stayed. Well, that ain't hit. We follered them tracks to a cave and after plannin' a little, Levi ventures in and he come out with the biggest bar yarn ye ever heard. "Thar's nineteen bar in thar if they's a one!" says he.

Well the cave was too narrow to do any shootin' in, so Levi says, "I'll jest go in and club 'em." He cut him a good healthy stick all right, but it wasn't long afore he came out faster than he went in! They was an awful tussle in thar o' some kind, fer Levi, he didn't look the same when he came out! His clothes were torn and he scratched up considerable. I had to laugh,

But Levi, he got mad. He's got plenty of temper anyhow, and he says "If'n you think you are so damned smart, just you go on in!" With that dare I went in. And gentlemen, bar was everywhar! Layin' around asleep. Nothing but bar! Hit smelled worse than any skunk den you was ever in. So I come out too; more than satisfied with what I seen.

When Ben emerged from the cave, Levi wryly asked him, "Didn't ye bring nairy a one with ye?" To which Ben replied, "No. And I hain't lookin' fer no bar fight neither!"

Parton said that Levi then armed himself with a bigger club and a knife, and he planned to enter the cave a second time. Ben continues with the story:

"I am going to git me a bar or else know the reason why" says Levi. I heard a scrimmage and a scramble and I never expects to see Levi again alive. The dust flew for Levi come out of thar directly dragging his bar, and if he wasn't tore up before, he was near that now. That bar was big all right and all bloody. If them bar hadn't been sleepy they would have et him alive. "Let's git another!" says I.

But Levi decided not to push his luck. He replied, "Hell! Git one your own self, I'm a going home! I know when I've got enough."

Though he sometimes used traps himself, for the most part Levi disdained their use. He particularly despised how some trappers carelessly placed them without marking them to warn humans. After one of his friends—an old blacksmith by the name of Huskey—froze to death after being caught in a bear trap on Blanket Mountain, Levi recalled, "These fellers as sets bar traps without marking them is doing the general public a injury. Them traps can be marked with a sourwood switch just as easily as not, but the plenty of them is jest too lazy and triflin' to take the trouble. They're jest too triflin' to live!"

Mason described Ben Parton as a "slight but wiry fellow with a deep, sonorous fog horn of a voice and a prominent Adams-apple." Ben lived not far from his friend Levi Trentham and they often hunted together.

Ben was a firm proponent of "still hunting" for bear and he felt that dogs were good for nothing but chasing deer or killing livestock. He particularly disdained North Carolina bear hunters and their Plott hounds, saying, "Ye don't never know what a damned Plott is going to do! They'll wag their tails while they're tearing ye to pieces. They're downright quare. What's more; them dogs has got the quarest names I ever heard of dogs having? Who in the hell ever heard of dog named John and Charlie? Them's no names fer dogs! They ought ter be named Lead, or Rover or Ranger. Them's dogs' names."

Parton felt strongly that a man who could not successfully "still hunt" didn't need to be in the woods at all. And like his friend Levi, he used traps, but he was wary of them. Ben said that he once set a trap near Laurel Gap and he forgot exactly where it was. While searching the general area for the trap, he stumbled upon a four-hundred-pound bear caught in it and the angry bruin nearly took his leg off. Ben recalled, "I ain't thinkin' that I'm anywhere nigh a trap when chee-whop! went a bar's teeth just like a steel trap within a inch of my leg! Hit didn't miss me far! The hair jest riz up all over me! Thet's the only time thet I was ever good and scared in these mountains and I have hunted a heap far and nigh too!"

Like most golden age hunters, Ben Parton continued to use the old-time Smoky Mountain rifle well after modern guns were popular, and he was vocal in his preference of muzzleloaders. He told Mason, "I'd rather have a good muzzle-loader because I'm used to thet. Ye can't shoot so fast, but ye won't overkill yer self."

Ben also bemoaned how city dwellers with their high-powered rifles and high-powered whiskey were ruining hunting in the mountains for local residents. He said, "I'm sort of like Levi and the other fellers. Don't kill more than ye can tote and don't drink no more than ye can walk under with a gun. Thet's the way ter have game a plenty fer all and safety too!"

In other words, a good hunter should kill only what he needs to survive and liquor has no place on a hunt. Well said, Mr. Parton.

Wiley Oakley

Wiley Oakley was the youngest and probably the most famous of all thcse East Tennessee hunters. Oakley made the most of his fourth-grade education, and he packed a lot of living into his sixty-nine years. He wrote two charming, unedited books about his life, and he served as a guide to many celebrities such as World War II journalist Ernie Pyle and John D. Rockefeller. Wiley also helped lay out the boundary lines for the Great Smoky Mountain National Park when it was founded in 1934.

Wiley Oakley's story begins with his birth in an East Tennessee cabin at the foot of Mount LeConte on what is today National Park land. He was the son of a Scottish immigrant father and full-blooded Cherokee mother. When the Civil War started, the Oakley family took refuge in the Smoky Mountains, and it was here that Wiley's father met and married his Cherokee wife.

Wiley, the youngest of eight children, was born to the couple in 1885, and he proved to be a quick study to his father, who supported the Oakley clan by hunting and trapping. Wiley recalled that the clearing around the family homestead was filled with animal hides stretched in frames being tanned to sale. Unlike some Tennessee bear hunters, the Oakley family used hunting dogs and they especially treasured their two Plott hounds, Trail and Troop. Wiley's father had obtained the dogs in North Carolina and valued them so much that he steadfastly refused good trade offers for the canines—and it was good for Wiley that he did.

When Wiley was about five years old, he decided to take his first solo hunting trip. Unarmed, but confident that he would be protected by the family Plott dogs, he enticed the hounds to follow him by feeding them corn pone. After walking several miles, the dogs struck a game trail but eventually lost it. By nightfall, the boy was hopelessly lost. Wiley recalled that though he was scared and crying, he was determined to make the best of it, as he hunkered down for the night sandwiched between his two Plott hounds. Warm as toast, he wrapped his arms around them and went to sleep.

The boy awoke once or twice during the long night, but he was reassured that his dogs were by his side. One dog arose once during the night to drive off an animal that lurked nearby, but soon returned. About an hour before dawn, the Plott hounds suddenly jumped up and ran off barking into the night, leaving young Wiley terrified and alone. He was certain that the dogs had been scared off and had left him alone to fend for himself. However, that was not the case. Instead, the dogs had heard a nearby search party and they had gone to lead the rescuers back to Wiley, saving his life.

This incident did nothing to deter the lad's love for the woods. At the tender age of eight years old, Wiley had already mastered the art of shooting an old-time Smoky Mountain rifle, and he regularly hunted and trapped with his father. By the time he was sixteen, Wiley had harvested untold numbers of deer, bear, turkey, rabbits, coons and squirrels. The youngster knew the Great Smokies like the back of his hand.

Wiley married at age nineteen. He and his family lived in several homes deep in the East Tennessee side of the Smokies—beautiful places with intriguing names such as Panther Branch, Wildcat Hollow, Scratch Britches Mountain and Cherokee Orchard. Wiley supported his wife and twelve children by farming, hunting and by offering his services as a guide to both hunters and tourists.

After he had been hunting and guiding in the Smokies for years, the National Park Service enlisted Wiley's help in laying out boundary lines for the new park. Though it eventually forced his family to move out of the

Wiley Oakley. *Courtesy of Great Smoky Mountains National Park Archives.*

park to nearby Gatlinburg, the coming of the park opened up a whole new chapter in Wiley's life. He soon became a celebrity of sorts, leading tourists on hikes to Mount LeConte. He became known as the "number one guide in the Smokies." The National Park Service even awarded him a badge with that inscription.

With his expert woodsman skills, his good looks, engaging personality, harmonica playing and witty stories, Wiley Oakley literally came to symbolize "the human side" of the Great Smoky Mountains. The National Park Service and local chamber of commerce sent him nationwide as their representative to entice visitors to the region, and it was a job that suited him perfectly.

In his books, which were both published unedited in his own vernacular and phonetic spelling, Wiley spun hunting yarns similar to an older version of Huckleberry Finn. But like Mark Twain, it was his humorous anecdotes that were the most delightful—and sometimes insightful. When asked if he had ever been lost, Wiley replied, "I never been exactly lost, but I have been bothered for two or three days a few times. But I got out. If I hadn't, I wouldn't be here today."

Wiley liked to refer to himself as the "Roaming Man of the Smokies," and he explained the advantages of having two names: "I like to have two names, kind of like a movie star, my own name and the Roaming Man. That way, if something bad happens, I can always put it off on the other feller."

Wiley told of a bear that had plagued his community for some time, killing livestock, destroying crops and robbing beehives. Try as they might, no one was able to kill or trap the outlaw bruin. However, one day a friend of Wiley's suggested that they fill up a bucket with a mixture of moonshine liquor and sourwood honey and leave it near the beehives and a cornfield.

A day or so later, they approached the hives and found that the "honey" bucket was empty. An uneven bear trail led into the cornfield. Soon they found signs that the bear had stumbled and rolled off down the hill, intoxicated. Wiley said that they went to the bottom of the hill and found the bear passed out "just as drunk as a fool." The bear was easily disposed of in its drunken stupor and it was of no further problem to the locals.

However, the most amazing thing to me about Wiley Oakley was his insight as a sort of "natural naturalist." All of these golden age hunters were keen observers of the natural world—they had to be, their very lives depended on it. But Wiley seemed to appreciate the healing qualities of time spent in the wilderness more than most. He understood the unique restorative benefits of living *with* nature and enjoying its bounty, as opposed to trying to impose his will on it or trying to control it.

Between what he learned on his own while living in the forest and what he learned through his regular association with National Park officials, botanists and wildlife biologists, Wiley Oakley became a renowned naturalist in his own right. Or as he described it best:

> *In the outdoor life, I have had lots of experience. All I have ever known is the Great Smoky Mountains. Nature in the Great Smoky Mountains is a wonderful study. I advise every person just to take time to stroll out on some of these beautiful trails and every now and then take the time to look and listen. Take a deep breath and look things over. It don't make any difference how young or old that you may be. Time and money don't mean anything.*

Wiley Oakley died in November 1954 at the age of sixty-nine, one of the last, and probably the most famous, of all the Tennessee ridge runners of the golden age of hunting. All quotes pertaining to Oakley are from transcripts in the library of the Great Smoky Mountain National Park.

CHAPTER EIGHT

THE LAST FRONTIER

Even today Graham County, North Carolina, is a last frontier of sorts. This sportsman's haven remains a sparsely populated county, a majority of which is federal forest land, and it is the only county left in North Carolina without a four-lane highway running through it. Unlike many neighboring mountain counties, there is little conventional commercial tourism in Graham County—no casinos, ski slopes, amusement parks or tourist trap trinket shops are found here.

Instead, visitors come to Graham County for the solitude and scenic splendor of the region, as well as for the many outdoor activities that can be enjoyed here. It is a place where real mountain living and real mountain values can still be found and enjoyed—with all the usual modern amenities, but little of the commercialism so prevalent elsewhere.

However, there was a time back in the1800s when Graham County really *was* a last frontier. Graham wasn't even an officially chartered county until 1872, and many early maps show the region as "Uncharted Indian Territory." To some degree it was just that. But the few folks living here knew the terrain intimately and required no maps.

White settlers were slow to come here. But they eventually settled near the small band of Cherokee that had managed to stay in the Snowbird Mountains after tribal removal in 1838. These Snowbird Cherokee still held proudly to their traditional beliefs and they continue to do so today. Then and now, there are more full-blooded Cherokee in Graham County who fluently speak their native tongue than probably anywhere else in the country. Colonel Will Thomas was among the first white settlers here. He opened a store near the present-day site of Robbinsville High School in the early 1840s.

Gradually other settlers followed, so that by the end of the Civil War there were homesteads and farms scattered across the county. Most of these settlers were independent hunters looking not only for a better life, but also for a place with "elbow room" where they could hunt, farm, fish and generally live as they pleased with no outside interference. Most were good, God-fearing people, but it could still be a pretty rough place. So rough, in fact, that a community on West Buffalo Creek was named "Rough" for all the fights and shootings that occurred there. Another section of the county was known as "Long Hungry" for the hunters who were often lost and left hungry there for a long time.

Like many mountain counties, there are literally too many famous hunting families in Graham County to name them all. But a few stand out, and they deserve special mention. The Orr, the Lovin, the McGuire and the Denton clans were all early Graham County pioneer families, and they are all golden age hunting legends whose stories deserve to be told. However, before we examine these Graham County sportsmen, let's take a look at an event that greatly impacted the hunting culture of this region.

In 1908, an English company, Whiting Manufacturing, bought 5,429-foot Hooper Bald and most of the land around it in western Graham County. Hooper Bald was named for Enos Hooper, the first doctor in the county, and his descendants make up yet another family of renowned local hunters. Canadian George Moore was a business associate of Whiting Manufacturing who was given the rights to establish an almost 2,000-acre hunting preserve on Hooper Bald in 1908. By 1911, an elaborate hunting lodge with the first telephone in the county and a caretaker's cabin had been built there, as well as a large game lot. More than 1,500 acres were eventually fenced in to contain the hunting animals that were soon to arrive there.

Moore arranged for more than a thousand exotic and native game and domestic animals to be shipped to Andrews and Murphy, North Carolina, in the spring of 1912. From those locations the animals were hauled by wagons to Hooper Bald. This was no small feat. It took Captain Frank Swan of Andrews almost four months to transport the entire contingent across the rugged terrain. Most of the animals survived the trip, and by the autumn of 1912 eight buffalo, fourteen elk, fifteen Prussian boar, six mule deer, nine Russian bear, twenty-five North American black bear and hundreds of turkeys, pheasants and domestic stock had found a new home on Hooper Bald. And so, too, had Cotton McGuire.

Garland "Cotton" McGuire

Local boy Garland "Cotton" McGuire was only sixteen at the time, but he knew a good thing when he saw it. He immediately secured a job at the lodge; in fact, he helped build it. It proved to be the perfect job for an outdoorsman like Cotton. By 1920, the young man had been promoted to foreman of the preserve and had led some of the first guided boar hunts in the Southern mountains. This would prove to be a landmark moment in Smoky Mountain hunting history for two reasons. It provided a new big game animal for mountain hunters to pursue with their dogs, one that was even faster and often more dangerous than bear. But more importantly, when the majority of these boars escaped the preserve, they found their "dream" home in the Smokies, and the hogs have thrived here ever since. These boars and their descendants have proven to be a blessing and a curse to the region. They are a blessing for hunters who enjoy the sport of hog hunting, and a curse to farmers and property owners whose crops and land the boars ravage.

By 1924, George Moore had soured on the idea of owning a hunting lodge and he turned the place over to Cotton McGuire. By then, the majority of the animals on the preserve had escaped or been killed. In 1926, Champion Paper bought most of the land, but they kept Cotton on as a fire warden, and he retained some of the acreage himself.

Cotton raised most of his family on the Bald and lived there for almost thirty years. He is generally agreed to have been the foremost hog hunting guide in the Great Smokies, as well as a fine all-around sportsman. Cotton was a voracious hunter and was good friends with other noted local hunting clans such as the Denton family. He is included in many early Graham County hunting photos and he clearly was a well-liked and well-respected man. Cotton McGuire continued to actively hunt and guide until his death at the age of sixty-two in 1957. Jim McGuire, one of Cotton's children, continues the family hunting tradition today, and the McGuire family still owns property not far from where they grew up on Hooper Bald.

Will Orr

Another renowned clan of big game hunters was the Orrs. The Orr family first came to Graham County from South Carolina sometime shortly before the Civil War. But it was not until after the conflict that their legend truly began.

After serving in the Union army during the Civil War, brothers Dave and George Orr used their military mustering out money to purchase a large parcel of land in the Slick Rock area of Graham County near Big Fat Gap. This region soon became known as the Dave Orr Mountains, and it was home to some of the finest big game hunters in the Southern highlands. Even today many members of the Orr family carry on that tradition. But these golden age Orr hunters were really something special. For example, Bart Orr killed fifty-seven bears in his hunting career, the last one when he was eighty-six years old. Jim and David Orr were also notable huntsmen, as were George, Andy and Lee Orr. But probably the best of the Orr clan was Will "Little Will" Orr.

If Cotton McGuire was the best hog hunting guide in the Smokies, then surely Little Will Orr was a close second. Little Will was born in the East Buffalo section of Graham County in 1889. He was the son of George Orr, and he was taught to hunt as a boy by his father and by his Uncle Dave. Though he was later to become exceptionally well-known as a hunting guide, Little Will Orr was almost as famous for his liquor-making abilities. Like fellow golden age hunter and distiller Quill Rose, Will Orr made no apologies for his moonshining either. He is reported to have once said that liquor making "was more profitable and a hell of a lot easier than working behind a plow for ten cents a day." But unlike Rose, Will Orr did serve some time in prison—a year and a day—for his illegal distilling of spirits. But, he took it all in stride, and he always remained a man of good humor and a welcome addition to any hunting party—both for his wit and for his hunting talents.

Little Will did whatever it took to support his family. In addition to liquor making, he sold ginseng, farmed, logged and worked construction on the Cheoah and Santeetlah dam projects. But Orr found his true calling working as a hunting guide. He began to work regularly as a guide once the boar began to escape from the Hooper Bald Preserve in 1912, and he continued to lead boar and bear hunts in the Smokies for the next forty years.

Little Will's hunting dogs were almost as famous and unique as he was. He especially favored a half-Plott and half-Redbone mix that usually resulted in a gritty, solid black hound with brindle trim. Little Will felt that his dogs were the best big game hunting dogs around, and few could argue with his results. Orr and his dogs killed thirty-one bears in one season in the Hazel Creek, North Carolina watershed, and they killed seven boars in only one month in November 1946.

In his 1947 book *Hunting and Fishing in the Great Smokies*, Jim Gasque refers to Will Orr as "having been one of the best hunting guides in the mountains for the past thirty years." Gasque was in awe of his stamina and noted that at the age of fifty-eight, Little Will could still "out-tramp" any younger man. Gasque added that "more often than not kills are made when Orr is in charge and he knows the hog country as well as any living man."

Will Orr continued to hunt until he was past eighty years old. After that he served as an advisor and mentor to younger hunters and often entertained his family and friends with his colorful stories until his death in 1983 at the age of ninety-four. Little Will Orr is still remembered fondly today as a mountain hunting icon of the last frontier.

The Lovin Family

The Lovin clan first came to Graham County after the Civil War, settling in both the West Buffalo and Big and Little Snowbird sections of the county. Like the Orrs, the Lovin family was well-known for its fine hunting dogs. The Lovin hounds were purebred Plott dogs that the family had evidently obtained from Montraville Plott in the mid-1870s. Lovin family descendant Marshall McClung recalls the Lovin dogs were dark brindle in color, and that they were known for "having plenty of nerve."

The earliest known photo of a Plott hound was taken at the Sam Lovin homestead about 1879. A closer examination of this picture reveals not only two fine specimens of old-time Plott hunting dogs, but also a superb portrait of two hard-hunting families—the Lovin clan and their friends the Sneeds. Look at the scores of hides, turkey beards and antler racks adorning the porch of the Lovin home. Moreover, look at the weathered faces of these seasoned mountain families. This is a classic example of a picture being better than a thousand words.

Sam Lovin and his sons—Blake, Rip, Tillman and Jake—were all master hunters who kept their dogs near the porch and their guns by the door, ever ready to strike a game trail. Probably the best known of the Lovin hunters was Joe Lovin. He was born about 1860 in Cherokee County, North Carolina, but as a young man relocated to Graham County to find work as a logger. He lived in the forks of Big and Little Snowbird Creeks and used that as his base of operations to become one of the best bear hunters in Graham County. Joe killed ninety-one bears in his hunting career—eighty-nine with his muzzleloading rifle and two with an axe. His flintlock rifle misfired on him twice due to wet gunpowder, so he was forced to kill two angry bruins armed only with an axe. He managed to walk away from those fights with no serious injuries, but that was not the case when he was later severely injured after being caught in a bear trap. The old hunter was stuck in the trap for several hours and nearly bled to death before finally managing to free himself and crawl for help.

The home of Samuel Blake Lovin, built in 1854 on Big Snowbird Creek in Graham County, North Carolina. *Left to right*: Jake Lovin, Osco Sneed, Sam Lovin, Grady Lovin, Lavina Lovin, Rip Lovin, Ollie Lovin, Bessie Lovin and Jack Lovin. The dogs on the far right and far left are Lovin family Plott hounds. This photo, taken in 1879, is the earliest known picture in existence of Plott hunting dogs. *Courtesy of Marshall McClung.*

But even that could not keep a good man down for long. Joe Lovin eventually recovered, and he continued to hunt big game and perpetuate his legacy as a golden age legend until shortly before his death at the age of ninety-eight, in 1958.

John Hamilton Chastain Denton

There are thousands of legends in Smoky Mountain hunting history. Only a few—the best of the best—are included in this book. It would be almost impossible for anyone to name the all-time best hunting clan in the history of the region. But if I had to pick the most prestigious group of sportsmen to ever roam these storied mountains, my vote would go to the Denton family of the Little Santeetlah and Little Snowbird sections of Graham County.

The true story of the Denton family is better than the best historical fiction ever written. They first came to America around 1630, and Denton descendants fought in the Revolutionary War, the War of 1812 and the Civil War—which is where our story really begins, with John Hamilton Chastain Denton.

John H.C. Denton shortly
after the Civil War.
Courtesy of Leota Wilcox.

John H.C. Denton was born in 1840 in north Georgia, but he grew up in
Benton, Tennessee. He was a giant of a man, with over two hundred pounds
of muscle packed on a six-foot, five-inch frame. He was well-known for his
feats of Herculean strength, as well as his willingness to put local bullies in
their place. John was a man who respected others, but who demanded that
same respect in return—and he had no problem getting it.

He loved the outdoors and was an expert woodsman with unusual skills.
Not only was he a crack shot, but he could also kill more small game with
rocks than most hunters could with a rifle or shotgun. As a lad, John had
developed an uncanny accuracy in hurling rocks, and it was a skill that he
utilized his entire life hunting with great success—and a skill that one day
would save his life.

After the Civil War broke out, John and his two younger brothers joined
the Confederate army on March 6, 1861. John fought at the Battle of First
Bull Run and at Cumberland Gap, and also served as part of a rear guard
for Confederate President Jefferson Davis on his retreat from Richmond,

Virginia. Coincidentally, John Denton's wife, Albertine, was a cousin of Jefferson Davis.

John also fought at the siege of Vicksburg and was taken prisoner there when the city surrendered to Union forces in July 1863. He was paroled under the condition that he would not continue to fight against the Union, but ever the defiant rebel, he returned to his Confederate unit in August 1863. John's younger brother Jeffery was killed in action sometime early that fall. John was devastated by the loss and returned the body of his brother to his grieving parents in late October of 1863. John remained in Benton, Tennessee, until the war ended.

But the war never really ended for John Denton. Not only had he lost a brother while fighting valiantly for a losing cause, but he came home only to be ostracized by his neighbors, some of whom had fought for the Union army. The only place that he could find any real solace was in the woods hunting and fishing, but most of the good game lands were gone too. Many other Confederate veterans had escaped to a better life in the far west. But with a wife and five young children, John Denton instead chose another option. He decided to head east, on a shorter and faster trip, to the last frontier of Graham County, North Carolina.

In 1870, the Denton family packed their wagon and crossed the Little Tennessee River at Calderwood. They then climbed over Carver's Gap as they entered Graham County, North Carolina. There were no roads—only game trails and primeval wilderness—but Denton liked what he was seeing as he forged deeper into the mountains. John literally chopped a road into what is now the Joyce Kilmer Memorial Forest. He found a slight clearing near Rattler Ford on Little Santeetlah Creek in the middle of giant old growth timber and decided that this would be their new home.

The Dentons were one of only about thirty-five white families in Graham County in 1870, and they were the *only* white people to ever live in what is now the Joyce Kilmer Memorial Forest. Their closest neighbors were a handful of Cherokee who lived a few miles away and valued their privacy as much as John Denton. Best of all, it was virgin wilderness with plenty of fresh water and abundant with fish and game. In short, it was a perfect place for the grizzled war veteran.

But now the real work began. First John had to find shelter for his family. He hollowed out a huge fallen chestnut tree for his family to live in while he worked on their cabin. This "tree house" had space enough for two rooms, and John could stand fully upright in it without touching the "ceiling." They lived happily in this enormous log until their cabin was finished—and what a cabin it was. John was a superb axe man. He carefully cut and precisely fitted the chestnut logs together. He further secured them with two-inch locust wood pins. The cabin was so well built that when the National Forest Service decided to demolish it in the 1940s, even a bulldozer could not fully tear it apart. Legend has it that it was knocked off its foundation, but the cabin held together as it rolled down a hill like a basketball. Finally it was dismantled after four days' work, by prying one log loose at a time.

Once his home was finished, John cleared almost twenty more acres so that the family soon had one of the finest farms in the region. He had the best of both worlds—a self-sufficient farm filled with fruit trees, vineyards, livestock and crops situated in the middle of his own private hunting and fishing paradise. Never one to waste anything, John continued to hone his rock throwing skills. He is said to have harvested record amounts of turkeys, pheasants, squirrels and rabbits with rocks to preserve lead and powder. But he did use his muzzleloading Civil War rifle to hunt big game, and he was a mighty bear hunter. However, he cared nothing for keeping a tally of his kills. He enjoyed hunting, and all of his sons were fine hunters as well. But John Denton and his family, like many golden age legends, were more focused on survival than scorekeeping.

John was a man of remarkable strength and stamina. He made four trips to Virginia *on foot* to bring back apple trees so his family could annually taste the fruit that he had enjoyed there during the war. He once cut and split over one thousand eight-foot-long chestnut fence rails in less than two days. Sometime in the 1870s, he made a 150-mile round-trip hike to Plott Valley to get some Plott bear dogs from his friend Montraville Plott. Thus began a love affair with the Plott hound breed that generations of Denton family members would share.

John treated his dogs like family and enjoyed their company wherever he went. He never tied his dogs and they obeyed his every command. John was known to even let his hounds stay in the house by the fire, and he would give a tongue lashing or a beating to anyone who mistreated them. John and his bear dogs forged an unusual bond that was repeatedly strengthened on many strenuous and successful bear hunts.

The Denton family flourished on Little Santeetlah Creek. John and Albertine eventually added four more children to their brood, bringing their total to five boys and four girls. Charlie, one of the Denton boys, recalled a joyous childhood hunting and fishing with his father, his siblings and their Cherokee playmates. Many relatives of these Cherokee children had been witness to or had endured the terrible Trail of Tears removal in 1838. They often shared their poignant stories with the lad, and as an adult he grew up to work as an advocate for the tribe with the Department of the Interior.

John sympathized with the tribe too, perhaps feeling a kinship to them as a Confederate veteran vanquished by the Union. Maybe he felt the need to somehow go "native" himself in a show of support for his neighbors. Or maybe, like the Biblical Samson, he felt his long hair had something to do with his strength; no one knows for sure. For whatever reason, as he grew older, John let his hair and beard grow to great lengths. His hair was kept plaited in two braids, both reaching well below his chest, and his beard stretched almost to his waist. With his colossal size and strength combined with his piercing blue eyes and lengthy locks, John Denton left a striking impression on anyone crossing his path—especially when accompanied by a pack of his loyal dogs. By 1885, he was a well-known and well-respected man in Graham County. More importantly, he had finally found the peace and inner happiness that had eluded him for so long while living in Tennessee after the war. John Denton had finally found a home.

All of these achievements and unique character traits would make John Denton a man worthy of inclusion on any list of golden age hunters. But it was his infamous 1892 tax fight that made him a true mountain legend. John was about fifty-two years old in 1892 when he made the twenty-mile walk

John H.C. Denton family at their home on Little Santeetlah Creek in what is now the Joyce Kilmer Memorial Forest about 1890. *Top row, left to right*: Arthur Denton, May Denton Rice, Molly Denton, Baxter Cook. *Bottom row, left to right*: John Hamilton Chastain Denton, Albertine Denton, Melissa Denton, Forest Denton. *Courtesy of Leota Wilcox.*

to the county seat of Robbinsville to visit friends and pick up some supplies. Upon arriving there, John went to George Walker's General Store, where he was confronted by the county sheriff, who loudly accused him of not paying his taxes. John quietly replied that he had already paid his two-dollar tax bill, and that he had a receipt at home to prove it. Perhaps the sheriff was looking to make a name for himself—or maybe he was just foolish. But he made a big mistake in calling John Denton a liar.

This was an intolerable insult to his honor. Big John promptly knocked the sheriff to the floor with a blow from his mighty right hand. To his credit, the lawman quickly regained his footing, only to make another error when he pulled a Bowie knife on Denton and slashed off half his long beard. John was enraged but unarmed, so he grabbed for the first weapon he could find to defend himself. It was a cast-iron scale weight and Denton swiftly used it to render the sheriff unconscious.

Soon deputies and friends of the sheriff came to the lawman's defense. Two more men pulled knives on John. He grabbed them by the backs of their necks and bashed their heads together, knocking them cold as their knives clanged to the floor. A few others foolishly joined the fray. John disposed of them all with quick hammer-like blows as he made his way to the street. One of his victims staggered out of the store screaming for help and he was soon joined by reinforcements from the nearby courthouse.

Badly outnumbered, and armed with only a piece of stove wood in each hand, John efficiently struck down several more of his attackers. In a brief lull in the action, he noticed that there was a plentiful supply of rocks on the unpaved street. As the brawl resumed with still more men charging after him, John efficiently picked them off one by one with a machine gun–like barrage of well-aimed rocks.

Captain Nathan Phillips, a friend and fellow Confederate army veteran of Denton's, was an innocent bystander pleading for the gang to cease their attack. They paid him no heed and continued to take casualties as they did so. On a rare miss, John threw one rock with such velocity that it cracked the weatherboard siding of the store and ricocheted off the wall, hitting Captain Phillips in the back with enough force to knock him to the ground. The old soldier took three weeks of bed rest to recover. John later said that it was the only regret that he had regarding the fight.

As the dust slowly settled on the courthouse square, nearly thirty injured bodies lay scattered on the street and in Walker's Store. Only Big John Denton remained standing. He gathered his supplies and headed quietly back to his home on Little Santeetlah Creek. He was never charged with any crime, nor was he ever asked again about paying his taxes.

Cabin built on Little Snowbird Creek in the late 1800s by John H.C. Denton. *Courtesy of Leota Wilcox.*

About 1896, John Denton moved to Little Snowbird Creek to join his sons, Forest and John L., who were already living there. The Denton brothers eventually purchased almost one thousand acres of prime hunting land here. Always on the lookout for better hunting grounds and "more elbow room," John built a new home here for his wife and their three youngest children. The Dentons thrived here and John continued to enjoy life as a farmer and hunter.

Still a physical force at the age of sixty-seven, John was seriously injured in a 1907 logging accident that badly fractured his right leg. He received proper treatment, but when the morphine wore off, he was in such severe agony that he cut the splints loose himself. As a result, the leg healed crookedly and John was left a cripple. But not for long: John cut himself two walking sticks and taught himself to walk again. He soon resumed hunting and his twenty-mile hikes to visit friends, albeit at a slower pace than usual. Friends recall that he was always accompanied by his loyal Plott dogs, and that even fifty years after the war he remained loyal to the Confederacy. Despite his affliction, the old warrior would still jump to his feet and emit a piercing Rebel yell anytime "Dixie" was played.

John Denton remained an active woodsman until his death in 1913 at the age of seventy-three. He is buried in the mountains where he finally found peace—the last frontier of Graham County. The old hunter left behind a long list of amazing accomplishments, but none more so than his children and their descendants, who perpetuated his hunting legacy on the last frontier. John and Albertine Denton can rest peacefully in their Snowbird graves with the knowledge that all of their nine children and their descendants grew up to be successful adults. But three of these Denton men would become exceptional hunting legends in their own right and they are worthy of inclusion on our exclusive list of golden age sportsmen. They are Forest Denton, John "Cub" Denton and Victor Denton.

Chalmers Forest Denton

Forest Denton, the son of John and Albertine Denton, was born in a wilderness paradise on Little Santeetlah Creek in 1875. He took to the woods like a duck to water and soon grew to be a woodsman to rival his legendary father. As a teen, the boy had his heart broken by a local girl and vowed never to marry. He never did, instead choosing a life devoted entirely to hunting and working outdoors.

Like his father, Forest was a big, strong man with craggy, weathered features and huge, brawny hands. He was a clean shaven fellow with a gruff, but keen sense of humor and a booming laugh. He almost always had a chaw of apple chewing tobacco in his jaw as he amused friends with his latest hunting stories.

About 1895, when he was twenty years old, Forest went to work for the Waldo Ranch on Little Snowbird Creek. Connecticut brothers Frank and Leonard Waldo hired him as caretaker of their cattle farm there. Forest liked the job and the location and was soon joined by his brothers Cub and Charlie. Forest bought a tract of land, and his parents and three youngest siblings moved to Little Snowbird around 1896.

Though he was an expert cattleman and well versed in most aspects of animal husbandry, Forest never rode a horse. He preferred the "shoe leather" express, as he tramped the hills on foot accompanied by his hunting dogs. He inherited a love of the Plott breed from his father and later in his life he bear hunted often with Mont Plott's boys Von and John Plott, as well as with other golden age hunting legends like Sam Hunnicutt and Granville Calhoun. Like most of these men, it was nothing for Forest to cover fifteen miles or more in a day over some of the most rugged terrain in the Southern mountains.

Between 1907 and 1917, Forest and his brothers accumulated about one thousand acres of land on Little Snowbird Creek. This became known as

Forest Denton in the late 1950s. *Courtesy of Leota Wilcox.*

the Denton Preserve, a place where the Denton family invited select friends from around the Smokies to hunt and fish. Forest prospered here, living alone with his dogs, hunting and fishing as he pleased. In the early 1900s, Forest Denton was hired as the county game warden. Even today this is no easy job, but back then on the last frontier it was similar in a lot of ways to being a sheriff in the Old West. Some citizens of Graham County moved there to get away from the law, and even the law-abiding residents felt it was their right to hunt when and where they pleased.

As one of the most respected hunters in the county, and because he was honest to a fault, Forest was the ideal man for the job. Local folks soon learned that Forest Denton would strictly enforce all game laws and that he cut no one any slack—not even himself. One Sunday afternoon he was out looking for poachers when he came upon some bear sign near a hollow tree. Forest rammed his walking stick into the tree and a huge bear charged out at him.

In self-defense, Denton had no choice but to shoot and kill the bruin. Forest could easily have walked away and never said a word about the incident—and who would have blamed him? But instead, he walked into Robbinsville and turned himself in for killing a bear out of season, and he paid his fine.

Forest had a mysterious gift for catching live rabbits without using a snare or trap of any kind. Once while searching for cattle with Cotton McGuire on Hoopers Bald, Denton returned to their camp with a full-grown rabbit squirming in the pocket of his hunting jacket. When asked how he did that, Forest replied, "Well, if I told you how I caught the rabbit you would say I was lying and I don't want anyone questioning my word." And they never did, as the old hunter took his secret to his grave.

Forest Denton lived happily on the Denton Preserve for the remainder of his long life; he died there in 1966 at the age of ninety-one. Even though he never had children of his own, I suspect that the grizzled old gamekeeper would be happy knowing that his great-nephew Thomas Denton Wilcox has restored his homeplace, and that he lives there with his family today. Moreover, I think he'd be pleased at how Tommy, his mother Mrs. Leota Wilcox and other Denton family members still proudly live and gather on Little Snowbird Creek for annual family reunions. It is a sacred place where

Original Forest Denton home on Little Snowbird. It is now renovated and owned by his great-nephew Thomas Denton Wilcox. *Courtesy of Leota Wilcox.*

they can enjoy sharing their rich heritage in the same scenic atmosphere once enjoyed by their forefathers.

John "Cub" Denton

John Llewellyn "Cub" Denton's life was unfortunately much shorter than that of his younger brother Forest—but it was a life no less colorful. Unlike Forest, who was born there, John L. did not arrive on Little Santeetlah Creek until he was nine years old in 1879. He quickly made up for lost time by finely honing his woodcraft as he roamed the mountains with his siblings and their Cherokee playmates. By the time he was a teenager, John L. was as skilled a hunter as men twice his age.

On one of his bear hunts, he mistakenly killed a mother bear with two sickly bear cubs. He was appalled by his error, as it violated the mountain bear hunter's code of never killing a sow with cubs. So the lad took the orphaned baby bruins back home and nursed them back to health. Soon the boy had the bears as

Baxter Cook on left and Forest Denton holding bear cubs that were the pets of John L. "Cub" Denton. *Courtesy of Leota Wilcox.*

domesticated as the family Plott dogs, which strangely seemed to enjoy their company. The young bruins imitated the hounds and followed the youngster everywhere he went. The bears enjoyed swimming with the lad and would playfully wrestle with him when he told them it was time to return home.

John L. fashioned leashes for the young bears, and he often took them to Robbinsville, where he would buy them sugar cubes in the general store. On one visit the cubs managed to get loose, and they emptied the store as they headed to the counter to get some treats by themselves. Order was restored when their young master came to retrieve his pets, which were now almost fully grown. Denton's Cherokee neighbors were amazed at the boy and his bears. They dubbed him with the nickname "Cub," and it was a name that stuck with him the rest of his life. Nearby Cub Gap, where he would later live with his wife and their first child, is named after him.

John L. "Cub" Denton bear hunt at Panther Flats, Big Snowbird, 1906. Cub Denton is on the far left. *Courtesy of Leota Wilcox.*

In 1886, when he was sixteen, Cub took a job as a lumber herder for Bemis Lumber Company. It was a dangerous job that required the boy to break up log jams as timber flowed downstream to Maryville, Tennessee. Using all of the skills he had mastered while running the ridges bear hunting, Cub excelled at the job.

By 1894, Cub and his small family had joined his brothers Forest and Charlie living on Little Snowbird Creek. Cub and his wife had seven more children there. It was a happy time for the Denton brothers as their father and mother eventually built a home there too. The Denton clan delighted in the superb hunting and fishing that could be found in their new homeland.

Cub was sick much of the last ten years of his life, and he eventually died of a ruptured appendix in 1911, at the age of forty-one. It is interesting to speculate as to what this golden age hunter could have achieved had he lived a longer life. But all of his children, particularly his son, Victor, carried on his love for hunting and the great outdoors.

Victor Denton

Victor "Vic" Denton was one of the first generation of the Denton clan born on Little Snowbird Creek. His childhood wasn't an easy one, but the boy

John L. "Cub" Denton. *Courtesy of Leota Wilcox.*

loved it there. His father Cub died when the lad was only nine years old, and his mother had difficulty taking care of eight children alone. Victor and his brother Horace were sent to a children's home in Goldsboro, North Carolina, where they stayed for two long years. The Denton brothers—already fine young mountain hunters—hated the humid flatlands of Piedmont North Carolina. They vowed to return home as soon as possible. Eventually they were able to do so, and they quickly resumed their life of hunting bliss on the last frontier of Graham County.

In 1924, Victor Denton was hog hunting on the Denton Preserve when he encountered a descendant of the original Prussian boars that had escaped from Hooper Bald. Vic and his Plott hounds struck a hog trail and chased the boar up and down a mountain ridge before finally baying it inside a hollow tree. Not having a clear shot, Vic decided to try and catch the boar. Just as he leaned his rifle against a tree, the hog charged madly at him. Thinking fast, Vic tried to jump over the boar as it ran between his wide-spread legs, with his dogs following close behind. His agility saved his life, but not before the hog had slashed a considerable amount of flesh from each of Vic's limbs. Unbothered by his wounds, he grabbed his gun, followed the hog trail and quickly dispatched the pig.

This was only one of the many memorable outdoor adventures experienced by Victor Denton. In 1936, he and Horace Denton, among others, were hired as "timber cruisers" by the National Park Service. The agency was recruiting elite mountain woodsmen to cover 500,000 acres of the newly proposed Great Smoky Mountains National Park to estimate the amount of timber on the property. It was a mission of great importance, as their estimates had to be accurate so they could stand up in court in the event that the state or federal purchasing of land for the park required condemnation action.

Vic and Horace would later scoff at allegations of those who believed there were many parts of the Smokies that had never heard the voice of a white man. The Denton brothers knew better. For more than two years they lived off the land, hunting and fishing in backcountry camps as they scoured every inch of this rugged wilderness. It was a job well suited for golden age hunting legends and the Denton boys did it well, completing the task in the fall of 1939.

Perhaps inspired by his Uncle Forest, Vic was hired by the North Carolina Wildlife Commission in 1939. He worked in various positions across the Smoky Mountain region during his twenty-year career, and he later served for fifteen years as manager of the Santeetlah Wildlife Refuge. Like his uncle, Victor's impeccable character and masterful hunting skills quickly earned him the respect of the local hunting community. In November 1951, Vic led war hero General Jonathan Wainwright on a boar hunt in the game refuge.

A story was written about the hunt in the March 1952 issue of *Outdoor Life Magazine*. Vic delighted in hunting with the ex–World War II prisoner of war, and he was particularly pleased that the general was able to bag a hog on the hunt.

But it wasn't just the Denton men who loved the great outdoors—so, too, did the Denton women. Vic's daughter, Mrs. Leota Wilcox, remembers her first and *last* "bear hunt." Some of her earliest memories are of hearing exciting hunting tales and of her two favorite family Plott dogs, Cap and Ranger. When she was about five years old, the little girl decided to go on a bear hunt of her own. After all, she was a Denton, and that's what Dentons did.

Leota summoned her dog Cap and headed for the woods. She and Cap walked until almost nightfall and the child was exhausted. But she wasn't scared and found a hollow log to hunker down in for the night. She and Cap curled up in the log and were both soon sound asleep. Meanwhile, back at the Denton homestead, her mother was beside herself with worry. She first

U.S. Army Lieutenant General Jonathan Wainwright with Victor Denton at Santeetlah Wildlife Refuge, November 1951. *Courtesy of Leota Wilcox.*

Leota Wilcox, age five, and her dog Cap. *Courtesy of Leota Wilcox.*

went to Forest Denton's nearby home, thinking the child may have been there, but to her dismay she wasn't. It was then that Mrs. Denton noticed her daughter's other favorite dog, Ranger, running back and forth between her and a nearby trail. Following the dog's lead, Ranger took Mrs. Denton straight to where her daughter and Cap were sleeping. While relieved to find her beloved child, Mrs. Denton was angry, too. Leota recalls that her mother took her home and "gave me the best whipping I ever got." Today Mrs. Wilcox continues to cherish her life on Little Snowbird Creek, although she has permanently retired as a bear hunter.

For all his well-deserved sporting accolades, Vic Denton is remembered first and foremost as a family man. Granddaughter Donna Wilcox Lewis remembers her grandpa Victor this way: "He was a man with values and he lived by them. My grandfather loved God, his family, hunting, fishing, friends, the good earth and good food. He never lost sight of the things that were important to him and that were a big part of who he was."

A big part of who Vic Denton was and what he stood for was the magnificent Denton Family Preserve on Little Snowbird Creek. Today over seven hundred acres of that land are still owned by the Denton family, who continue to proudly perpetuate the legacy of their ancestors on the last frontier of Graham County.

CHAPTER NINE

HAZEL CREEK AND DEEP CREEK: A SPORTSMAN'S PARADISE

Two Swain County tributaries—Hazel Creek and Deep Creek—and the region around them are still revered today by the thousands of anglers, hikers and campers who visit the North Carolina side of the Great Smoky Mountains National Park. But before the government claimed these watersheds for the National Park and Fontana Lake, Hazel Creek and Deep Creek were well-known as a sportsman's paradise for hunters and fishermen, both on a regional and a national level.

Hazel Creek was the site of record-setting bear hunts and the location of the legendary Hazel Creek Clubhouse, a cabin built by lumberman Jim Stikeleather for sportsmen to use as their base camp for adventures into the area that Horace Kephart tagged the "Back of Beyond." It was a place where St. Louis Cardinals baseball executive Branch Rickey contracted H.V. "Von" Plott to take him on what turned out to be an epic bear hunt. Rickey, best known for his role in integrating professional baseball with the signing of Jackie Robinson, was an avid bear hunter. In the fall of 1935, Rickey, accompanied by Von Plott and his nephew Little George Plott, as well as their friends Jim Laws, Bob Haynes, Oliver Laws, Taylor Wilson and others, embarked on a bear hunt that would jump twenty bears in just three days. Their party eventually killed a total of eight bruins, six in one day, supposedly a Hazel Creek record.

Deep Creek is a land steeped in mountain history and tradition. It was in this rugged region—near the mouth of Keg Drive Branch—that the Cherokee hero and martyr Tsali hid from United States soldiers during government removal of the tribe in 1838. And it was near here that the Cherokee chief Big Bear lived on a huge tract of land known as Big Bear's Reserve in the early 1800s. Both the Deep Creek and the Hazel Creek watersheds were favorite campsites of renowned outdoor writer Horace Kephart. Kephart

1935 Branch Rickey Hazel Creek bear hunt. Rickey is third from right and H.V. "Von" Plott is second from right. *Plott family collection.*

helped make both of these areas, as well as their local hunters, famous in his 1913 book *Our Southern Highlanders*.

But to truly appreciate Hazel Creek and Deep Creek for what they once were, we must go back in time a bit, to a time before the lumber companies, before the National Park Service, before the TVA and before Horace Kepahart. A time when old-time hunter Fate Wiggins recalled that only about eight or nine Indian and white families made their living hunting along the banks of Deep Creek and Indian Creek. It was a time when the region truly was a sportsman's paradise.

In my opinion, four Swain County golden age sportsmen have come to symbolize this earlier era better than any others. They are Mark Cathey, Acquilla "Quill" Rose, Samuel Hunnicutt and Granville Calhoun. These are their stories.

William Marcus "Uncle Mark" Cathey

William Marcus Cathey was born on Conley Creek near Whittier, North Carolina, on January 28, 1871. He spent the bulk of his adult life living as a bachelor with his sister or mother near Indian Creek, a tributary of Deep

Creek, about four miles north of Bryson City, North Carolina. He recalled living a simple but happy existence as a child in a log cabin with his five brothers and three sisters. The Cathey clan lived off the land—hunting, fishing and farming. It was not an easy life, but as an adult Mark said that "we will never be as prosperous again."

When Mark was twelve years old, he killed his first bear with a muzzleloading rifle that his father had given him. The lad was hooked, and from that point forward he devoted his life to hunting and fishing in his native mountains. During his lifetime he only briefly left Swain County three times, but he returned to make his living as a logger, hunter, trapper and hunting and fishing guide. When it came to living or working outdoors, no one did it better than Mark Cathey.

A friend once described Mark Cathey this way: "He was lean and lank, but not tall, and he was as tough as a mountain hickory. He was the nervous, wiry type. He had piercing eyes and there was an innate refinement and courtesy about him." Another unique feature about him was his unforgettable voice. Cathey's speech was remembered as sounding like "W.C. Fields with an Irish accent." His accent and his soft mountain drawl further enhanced Mark's sense of humor and his storytelling skills.

Mark Cathey's affable nature, combined with his superb hunting and fishing talents, resulted in the local residents of Swain County often referring to him as "Uncle" Mark. "Uncle" is a term of endearment that mountaineers sometimes bestowed upon respected elder male friends who were not blood kin. It was considered an honor to be called "uncle" and no one deserved it more than Mark Cathey.

Even today, more than a half a century after his death, Swain County folks still have their favorite anecdotes about Uncle Mark. Like the time he was caught in one of his own traps and said, "It wasn't such a good trap; otherwise I couldn't have got out." Others recall the time that Mark was first served raisin bran cereal, as he spit the raisins out and exclaimed, "By God, there's been a damn mouse in the bran!"

Granville Calhoun told of a time when their hunting party was stranded in a blizzard in the Hall cabin atop Thunderhead Mountain. When asked how cold it was outside, Cathey replied, "I can't rightly tell, when I hung the thermometer on the nail outside the door, the mercury dropped so fast that it jerked the nail right out of the wall."

Mark once described the steep terrain near Siler Meadow this way: "Some of these mountains are such that going up, you might near have to stand up straight and bite the ground, but going down, a man needs hobnails in the seat of his pants."

Swain County hunters and hunting dogs (Plotts and possibly Walkers) at the Bryson Place on Deep Creek, circa 1920s. Mark Cathey is fifth from right in plaid shirt. *Courtesy of Jim Casada.*

No one enjoyed the practical jokes often played in hunting camps better than Mark Cathey. Once while camped at Swan Meadows in nearby Graham County, Thad Bryson switched Mark's false teeth with those of another hunter while Cathey was asleep. The next morning Thad found Mark trying to adjust his teeth with his knife as he told Thad, "Ain't it funny, my damn teeth shrunk on me last night and I'm trying to make them fit." Thad admitted to Uncle Mark what he had done and they both got a big laugh out of it.

But Mark gave as good as he got, and he played a joke of his own on Thad while the two were bear hunting with a party on Proctor Creek. While sitting around the campfire, Thad complained to Cathey that his new boots were hurting his feet. Mark volunteered to wear them for Thad the next day to break them in. Thad agreed, and late the next day he saw Mark heading toward him barefoot, carrying Thad's boots. Mark exclaimed to Thad, "God almighty, why'd you give me these boots? I couldn't wear them at all. I cut out the toes and cut slits in the sides and they still hurt my feet. Here, you can have them back!"

But aside from his sharp wit, it is his hunting and fishing exploits for which Mark Cathey is best remembered. He was probably the finest hunter in the region. By his own account, he killed "a passel of bears," at least fifty-seven and maybe more. Cathey killed his biggest bear on the left-hand fork of Deep Creek near Bryson Place. Mark said the bear weighed over five hundred pounds field dressed, and that it took him five shots to bring the monster bruin down.

Cathey was a dedicated proponent of Plott bear dogs. He would hunt with no other hounds and kept Plotts until the day he died. Sam Hunnicutt confirmed this in his 1926 book, *Twenty Years of Hunting and Fishing in the Great Smokies*. Hunnicutt recalled three of the Plott dogs by name—Dread, Jolly and Old Wheeler—as well as Mark's intense dedication to them.

Uncle Mark was a notable turkey hunter too. He prided himself on his abilities to call gobblers in with his mouth, or by using only a green leaf. He disdained the use of artificial callers and decoys. His favorite turkey hunting weapons were either his old muzzleloading rifle or a .22-caliber rifle.

There are those who perhaps can offer credible arguments that there were better golden age hunters than Mark Cathey. But few can dispute the fact that he was the best all-around sportsman ever to live in the region, and he was without peer as a trout fisherman. Author Jim Gasque devoted an entire chapter to Uncle Mark in his 1948 book *Hunting and Fishing in the Great Smokies*. Gasque referred to Cathey as "the champion of champions of regional anglers" and "the greatest dry-fly fishermen in the Smoky Mountains."

Gasque was no slouch as a fisherman himself. He writes of intrepid anglers coming from across the United States to fish with Mark and to study his unconventional tackle and techniques. These visitors were awe-struck as they watched the master angler use an extra heavy leader and a yellow-bodied gray hackle fly to catch record amounts of trout. Moreover, they were amazed at his uncanny casting skills. Cathey had mastered the ability to skip-hop his fly across the water's surface, barely getting it wet, in a skittering, jittery dance that drove the fish wild. Gasque wrote that Mark had learned the secret "that trout could be excited into a striking fervor if one possessed the ability to dance the fly artfully over the fish." Gasque added that very few ever master this technique, but that Mark Cathey had "not only mastered it, he had perfected it." Mark's unorthodox gear, combined with his unconventional style, were often imitated, but never duplicated.

Mark Cathey was well-known as a modest and polite man, but he enjoyed showing up the outsiders who often initially made fun of him and doubted his abilities. Clad in overalls, with minimal fishing gear and a "chaw" of tobacco tucked firmly in his cheek, Uncle Mark was an easy target for these so-called experts. He would patiently wait until these uppity visitors grew frustrated as they exhausted their limited skills catching little or no fish. He would then ask them to let him borrow their worst fly. Then the show would begin as Uncle Mark would proceed to catch his limit in record time, using the very same fly that the "expert" visitor had just said wouldn't work.

Another time after being chastised by an "outlander" that his methods and tackle wouldn't work, Cathey responded, "Now remember, it ain't these 200 flies colored like a store window, but the man behind the rod—that's what counts."

Uncle Mark once watched in quiet amusement as an arrogant city slicker with state-of-the-art gear and a fifteen-inch Bowie knife strapped to his belt caught a miniature trout. The visitor excitedly shouted to Mark, "What do I do now?" To which Cathey replied, "Sir, climb out there on the end of that pole and stab that fish to death with your Bowie knife."

Stories abound of Cathey routinely catching enough trout to feed five men before camp could be set up and water boiled for coffee. He and his friends—all fine fishermen themselves—often had fishing contests, and Mark always won. Fate Wiggins recalled to folklorist J.S. Hall that he and Mark once had a daylong match on the head of Forney Creek. They caught 330 fish between them, with Fate catching 150 and Mark 180. Sam Hunnicutt and Cathey engaged in similar duels, but Hunnicutt always acknowledged that Mark was the superior angler.

By 1944, old age and heart ailments had slowed the old woodsman down. But Mark Cathey disregarded his doctor's orders and continued to hunt and fish. In August of that year, Mark accompanied Jim Stikeleather and another friend on what would prove to be his last fishing trip to Hazel Creek.

Using a walking stick to steady himself in the stream, the elderly angler put on a fitting curtain call to his fishing career. He caught fish after fish, including one huge trout that had avoided the party all day. As the sun was setting, Mark reeled the big fish in and told his partners, "Well, I'm through gentlemen." Uncle Mark Cathey had caught the last trout of his storied lifetime.

In October 1944, at the age of seventy-three, Mark Cathey took one of his Plott dogs with him back into the Smokies for a squirrel hunt. After not returning by dark, his sister became worried and a search party was sent to find him. Sometime after midnight, he was found sitting under a large oak tree, his rifle across his lap, dead from an apparent heart attack. Mark's loyal Plott hound was still by his side trying to keep him warm and protect him.

After learning of his death, his friend and hunting partner Granville Calhoun said, "Now there was a man who knew the Smokies like they were the palm of his hand. Mark was quite a character. He spent most of his life in the woods and that's the way he would have wanted to go."

Mark Cathey once wryly noted that he had been "accused of being the best fisherman in the Smokies." And there is no doubt in my mind that he was. But Uncle Mark Cathey was much more than that. In my opinion he was the best all-around sportsman ever to live in the Great Smoky Mountains. But just as importantly, Mark Cathey personified all the best qualities of the golden age hunting legends. He was a confident, capable, dignified and modest mountaineer, quietly proud of himself and his homeland—a place that he vowed never to leave again. And he never did.

Mark Cathey is buried in a pretty cemetery on School House Hill in Bryson City, North Carolina. His tombstone looks out over the Deep Creek watershed that he loved so well, and it fittingly reads, "Beloved Hunter and Fisherman—Was Himself Caught By the Gospel Hook Just Before the Season Closed For Good."

Samuel J. Hunnicutt

Samuel "Sam" Hunnicutt was born in 1880 in Yancey County, near Burnsville, North Carolina. When he was three years old, his family moved to Swain County, North Carolina, a place that he often referred to "as being in the suburbs of the Great Smoky Mountains." Remembering those days to writer Bob Terrell in 1958, Sam said that he knew of fifteen families there who made a living catching trout and selling them for a penny each.

Sam later made his home at the mouth of Hammer Branch on Deep Creek, and he lived there with his family until the National Park Service took their land in 1942. Like his friend Mark Cathey, Sam sometimes worked as a farmer and logger, but he devoted most of his life to hunting and fishing in the Deep Creek watershed of the Great Smokies.

However, Hunnicutt did not limit his outdoor pursuits just to this rugged area. He claimed the entire Smoky Mountain range as his personal game lands. He said that his hunting territory consisted of 300,000 acres and that it was 40 miles wide and 160 miles long. Few, if any, men knew this region better than Sam Hunnicutt.

Sam was a man of strong opinions regarding woodcraft, hunting and fishing—but he could back them up, and he often did. He referred to himself somewhat tongue-in-cheek as "the general manager of the Bryson

City branch of the Great Smoky Mountains tourist bureau." Sam claimed never to exaggerate in the telling of his hunting stories, but he had absolutely no problem in proclaiming himself "a perfect hunter and fisherman." And he was no doubt a great one—one of the all-time best.

Unlike many golden age hunters, Hunnicutt did not use a muzzleloading rifle. His weapon of choice instead was a modern-day .38-40 lever action Winchester rife. He preferred the Winchester because it "had a shocking power in the bullet" and it effectively killed game quickly and cleanly. Sam disdained the use of shotguns and traps because they were often inefficient and caused game to suffer needlessly.

Sam was passionate about hunting with hounds and, unlike some hunters of his era, who specialized their dogs on big game only, his dogs would hunt almost anything at his command. Coons, deer, squirrels, bear, boar and even otter and mink—the Hunnicutt hounds were truly multipurpose hunting dogs. Sam had very specific ideas in what he looked for in a hunting dog. First and foremost he wanted a dog that he could always depend on, that would obey his every command. He felt that only purebred dogs mixed once with another purebred hound could achieve that goal. By this Hunnicutt meant that his ideal dog would be a fifty-fifty cross of two specific purebred hounds. And not just any breed would do. His preferences were a Black and Tan and large beagle cross, or a Redbone and large beagle mix. Sam's favorite dog was a female Black and Tan–Beagle mix that he called Old Muse. She was a remarkable dog. Old Muse would not run farm stock unless instructed to do so, and she would stop in a dead run on a hot game trail to start another one, if Sam ordered her to.

Like Mark Cathey, Sam was an all-around sportsman. He was in on fifty-six bear kills, and he caught or killed more than one thousand raccoons and seventy-six foxes, along with untold numbers of pheasants, squirrels, turkeys, rabbits and other small game. Hunnicutt was probably second only to the master angler Mark Cathey in his fishing capabilities, catching literally thousands of native trout. But it should be duly noted that like all golden age legends, Sam ate, sold or gave away all of the game that he harvested. He wasted none of it and he would tolerate no one who did.

Hunnicutt often worked as a paid hunting guide. One of his customers, a New Yorker named Martin Eppley, repeatedly suggested to Sam that he should write a book about his hunting adventures. Sam finally did, and in 1926 his book *Twenty Years of Hunting and Fishing in the Great Smoky Mountains* was published. Outdoor writer Jim Casada, a Bryson City native, describes the book as "a quaint little volume," and he calls it "fascinating." However, he continues to state that Sam was certainly not a "literary giant, nor was he a polished writer." Casada adds that "on the other hand, once you have read his accounts, there is no doubt whatsoever that Sam was a mighty Nimrod."

I agree with Casada's assessments and I would further add that if taken at strictly face value, Sam's writing was at times repetitive and monotonous. His collection of stories is basically a journal or log of his life as an outdoorsman in the Great Smokies. After a while it can all sort of run together and sound the same. However, a closer examination of his work reveals its great value. Sam provides a clear snapshot of a bygone era and golden age hunters, the likes of which we will never see again. Just as importantly, he tells us a lot about himself and his hunting friends, as well as their extraordinary skills and stamina.

For instance, Hunnicutt clearly took good care of his dogs. He always made sure that they were properly watered, fed and, if need be, doctored before he took care of himself. Subtle mentions of cooking bread for his hounds, as well as making warm beds for them made from leaves and tree boughs, show the compassion that Sam had for his dogs.

Sam's minimalist woodcraft skills were superb and are reminiscent of the old-time long hunters. Unless serving as a guide, he traveled light, carrying only the bare essentials—rifle, ammo, knife, maybe a camp axe, a bedroll, some salt, flour, coffee and perhaps some potatoes or fruit. In no time he could set up a primitive but comfortable camp shelter, such as a lean-to made from bark or branches, and have a fire started. Within minutes after making camp, he could kill or catch his meal, and he could expertly cook a wilderness banquet on a creek-stone hearth, perhaps frying up some potatoes or whipping up some stone-baked bread as he brewed fresh coffee. But, if need be, Hunnicutt and his compatriots could travel even lighter, and they could literally live off the land, gathering native berries and plants, supplemented by game or fish.

Another interesting fact about Sam was his hunting partners. His casual mention of hunting with legends like Mark Cathey, Granville Calhoun, Forest Denton, Cub Denton, Davie Orr, Andy Orr, Dave Swann, Ed Hyatt, Mark Boone and Ike Whitson all indicate just how well-respected Hunnicutt was by his peers. After all, no less an expert than Daniel Boone once said that "a man should choose his hunting partners as carefully as choosing a wife." And rightfully so, because your very life can depend on the skills of your hunting partners. Clearly Sam Hunnicutt was highly regarded by a hall of fame roster of the best sportsmen in the Smokies.

While Sam was not shy about stating his obvious strengths as an outdoorsman, he was equally quick to point out his fears and mistakes.

Swain County hunters and bear dogs (Plotts and possibly Walkers and Hunnicutts), circa 1920s. Third from right is Sam Hunnicutt, holding a lead for his Hunnicutt hounds. Sixth from left, holding a lead for his Plott dogs, is Mark Cathey. *Courtesy of Jim Casada.*

Though it never slowed him down in the woods, he had no problem in admitting his deathly fear of rattlesnakes after having been bitten by one earlier in his career. He also readily admitted an error that he had once made that had cost the life of one of his prized bear hounds. Sam was undoubtedly a tough man, but he was sensitive to the feelings of his hunting partners. He was always careful never to openly criticize them or their dogs.

But perhaps the most impressive thing about Hunnicutt was his ability to cover huge amounts of rugged terrain in just a few hours. In his book, Sam casually mentions covering almost twelve miles in half a day on the headwaters of Nettle Creek, as well as similar distances high up the left fork of Deep Creek on Keg Drive Branch. He nonchalantly writes of a hunt above Bryson Place, where he walked nine miles, made camp and killed and cooked supper in less than four hours. This would be impressive in flatland forests, but Sam was routinely doing this in some of the steepest and roughest land east of the Mississippi River.

It should be noted that these skills were common in *all* the golden age hunters, not just Sam Hunnicutt. Most hunting stories—including Sam's—tend to focus primarily on the game that was harvested and not the work that went into harvesting it. The sportsmen took that for granted, as it was simply a way of life for them. This to me is the true value of Sam Hunnicutt's writing. Without even meaning to, Sam's book quietly illustrates the remarkable stamina of these amazing men and how physically difficult it was to hunt back then. Having hiked many of these areas myself, I am left in awe of their physical capabilities.

While Sam Hunnicutt will never be compared to Ernest Hemingway or even Horace Kephart for his writing skills, he has nevertheless left us with a worthwhile study of the golden age hunter. But even if he had never written a book, Sam Hunnicutt would be on the short list of Smoky Mountain hunting legends. However, the fact that he did, and the insight that his work provides us on these hunters, makes him even more important in the annals of Smoky Mountain hunting history. Moreover, it reminds us of an earlier era, a time when Deep Creek and Hazel Creek were truly a sportsman's paradise.

Acquilla "Quill" Rose

Acquilla "Quill" Rose was born on May 4, 1841, making him the oldest of this golden age quartet—and arguably the most colorful. The world's most gifted novelists or Hollywood screenwriters could never have created a character as interesting as the real-life Quill Rose.

Quill was a tall, handsome man, with long dark hair and beard and a broad-shouldered, muscular frame. Author Wilbur Zeigler once described Rose as "being good natured, but a desperate character when aroused." Like many old-time hunters, Quill would not tolerate slights or insults from anyone. Historian John Preston Arthur said that shortly after the Civil War Quill was shot during a dispute with a man named Rhodes outside of Bryson City, North Carolina. Rose, though seriously wounded, managed to pull a knife and kill his attacker.

Quill had clearly acted in self-defense, but to avoid possible prosecution, he hid out in Texas for a while. After a few years, he returned to the Smokies and he spent the remainder of his life here. Zeigler further wrote that Rose resolved to "recognize no authority and to live his life in a pure state of natural liberty." And by all accounts that is exactly what Quill Rose did.

Acquilla "Quill" Rose at home on Eagle Creek. *Courtesy of Great Smoky Mountain National Park Archives.*

The headwaters of Eagle Creek (above the Hazel Creek watershed) on a ridge straddling the North Carolina and Tennessee state lines was where Quill Rose made his home. He lived there with his Cherokee wife Vicie and their children, along with his brother Jake Rose and his family. This remote backwoods location proved to be the perfect home for the Rose brothers—a place for them to hunt, fish, trap, make liquor and, if need be, hide from the law.

Quill felt that it was his God-given right to make moonshine, and even though he was caught a time or two, it never seemed to slow him down much. Quill sold his liquor, which he referred to as "tanglefoot," for a dollar a gallon. He claimed to be the best distiller of spirits in the Smokies and often said that his "tanglefoot" was "as pure as the morning dew." Rose did not buy into the idea that whiskey was better if it was aged. He once said that he had drunk some of his liquor that was a week old and that it was no better than a batch fresh from the still.

Seymour Calhoun, the son of Granville Calhoun, told of a time when revenuers once surrounded the Rose homestead and told Quill that they had come to take him in. They warned him to come out quietly and surrender, with their guns aimed at his front door. Quill emerged from the cabin with his hands up and told the lawmen that he would indeed go with them. But Rose warned the posse that he doubted they would make it back home alive if he did. The posse would have to first get by his brother Jake and some of his other friends, who were waiting to ambush them somewhere along the trail. Quill quickly added that if they still insisted, he would gladly accompany them quietly without a fight—it was their choice.

The lawmen were at an impasse and struggled to decide what to do next. However, they quickly came to their senses. The agent in charge bought a jug of liquor from Quill, politely wished the old blockader good day and the posse hurried back to Bryson City.

Moonshiners are often depicted as sorry folks, but Quill Rose was anything but lazy. In addition to making liquor, he was a fine blacksmith and he also farmed, ran a gristmill and further supported his family by hunting and trapping.

There was a five-dollar reward on wolves in Western North Carolina up until 1891, and Quill collected more than his share of the bounty money. He often told the story of the time that he fell into "a wolf nest" hidden behind a waterfall on nearby Bear Creek. Rose had been searching for a sheep-killing wolf that had plagued local farms for three months. The wolf had been trapped once, but it had escaped by gnawing its leg off. Even with only three legs, the rogue wolf continued to raid farms and had evaded capture.

Quill said that he slipped and fell above the falls while hunting for the lobo, and that he somehow ended up "striking the bottom and landing on something soft and hairy." It turned out that not only had he had fallen into a wolf den, but he had landed on the three-legged sheep-killing canine itself. He continued with the story:

Thar I was a straddle of that varmint's back, and my fingers in the hair of its neck. Well, the wolf snarled and struggled like mad, but I had a holt of him. I didn't dare to lose my holt to git my knife, so I bent him down with my weight, and getting' his head in the water, I drowned him in a few minutes. Then I toted and dragged him out to the dogs. He had been living high off the settlements for months, til he war to fat to fight well.

Some have suggested that Quill took the credit of another lesser-known hunter who actually killed the three-legged wolf. Maybe so, but no one could have *told* the story any better than Quill Rose.

Quill further supplemented his income by digging and selling wild ginseng root. Once while bear hunting, he became separated from his hunting party and found the largest ginseng patch that he had ever seen—at least a few acres stretching across both sides of a hollow. He kept the secret to himself and vowed to return to it later alone. Much to his chagrin, he never managed to find it again as long as he lived. Ironically, before his death he mentioned roughly where he thought it was to Sam Hunnicutt. Sam writes in his hunting memoirs of finally finding it himself near Chimney Rock Branch.

Rose was a carefree fellow who liked the simple pleasures of life. He often rode a mule, and he sometimes took his fiddle along with him as he traveled the backwoods trails, singing and playing music for his own enjoyment. There are many stories of hunters and herders who were surprised to hear the loud, joyous singing and raucous fiddle playing of Quill Rose as he and his mule ambled down remote mountain paths.

Bear hunter Alphonso "Fonz" Cable told folklorist Joseph Hall a story regarding Quill and his mule. It seems that Rose was riding along one day when his mule began to continually kick one of his hooves into Quill's stirrup. Finally the mule knocked Quill's boot out of the stirrup and lodged its hoof into it. Rose supposedly said, "By God, if you want to ride so bad, then you can, I will just get off and walk." And that is exactly what he did, allowing the mule to hobble along a ways with one hoof in the stirrup. Fonz said it did not take the mule long to learn its lesson, and that Quill was soon back astride the jackass, riding happily along.

When the Civil War broke out, Quill joined the Confederate army. He served under Colonel Will Thomas and was one of the few white members of Thomas's Cherokee Legion. After the conflict ended Quill Rose's reputation as a renowned hunter became well established on both the regional and national levels. About 1881, when Quill was forty years old, authors Wilbur Zeigler and Ben Grosscup spent some time hunting and visiting with Quill. The writers would later devote almost an entire chapter to him in their 1883 book *The Heart of the Alleghenies: Or Western North Carolina.* Quill complained to the writers that game was getting scarce in the Smokies. He lamented that he had "only" been able to harvest ten bears that year, but in the past he had generally killed twenty or more in a season.

Before embarking on a hunt, the writers marveled at Mrs. Rose's ability to whip up a fine mountain breakfast and Quill's habit of enjoying a dram of whiskey before the meal. They also noted Quill's love for bear hunting, as well as his finely trained Plott bear dogs. The journalists wrote that Quill's hounds required no leash and that they responded only to his command. The writers concluded that Rose had "reduced the art of dog training to a fine art."

Legend has it that Rose once ordered two of his Plott dogs to wait for him at the depot in Proctor, North Carolina, while he visited friends in nearby Bryson City for a few hours. But Quill had a little too much fun in Bryson City and he ended up staying there for two days. When he finally returned to the depot, his loyal Plott hounds were still there, awaiting his arrival.

About 1906, Quill Rose began to bear hunt with another soon-to-be well-known journalist—Horace Kephart. Though Quill was in his mid-sixties by then, Kephart wrote admiringly of the vigor and skills of the elder hunter. Kephart's 1913 book *Our Southern Highlanders* has several colorful anecdotes about him. Though he sometimes hunted with a lever action Winchester, Rose told Kephart of his preference for muzzleloading rifles, as well as his disdain for modern-day weapons. Quill said, "I don't like them power-guns; you could shoot clear through a bear and kill your dog on the other side."

Quill continued to ardently bear hunt and make liquor until shortly before his death in 1921. In fact, he was arrested in 1912—but released with a warning—for making moonshine when he was seventy-one years old. When the judge asked him to state his plea, guilty or not guilty, the old bootlegger is said to have replied, "Maybe."

Like his Tennessee counterpart, Black Bill Walker, Acquilla "Quill" Rose was a man who lived his life on his own terms and made no apologies for it. He undoubtedly achieved his goal of living in a pure state of liberty and recognizing no authority. His passing marked the end of an era of freeborn mountain hunters, the likes of which we will never see again.

Granville Calhoun

Granville Calhoun—often referred to as the "Squire of Hazel Creek"—was born in 1875 in the Western North Carolina community of Wayside. The settlement was on the Little Tennessee River about twelve miles below Bushnell and twenty-five miles from Bryson City, North Carolina. Granville's father, Joshua Calhoun, moved the family to Hazel Creek in about 1884 when Granville was nine years old. The elder Calhoun carved the first wagon road into the region and brought the first wagon to Hazel Creek. Joshua Calhoun was a progressive thinking man and was responsible for establishing the first school and the first church in the area. Though it was still a wilderness then, a few settlers had already been living there for almost fifty years.

Moses Proctor, the first white settler in Hazel Creek, had come over from Cades Cove, Tennessee, in the early 1830s, and the community of Proctor was named for him. The Proctors were soon joined by a few other pioneer families, including one of the most prolific bear hunting clans in the Smokies—the Samuel Cable family. Two of Samuel Cable's grandsons, "Little" John and Alphonso "Fonz" Cable, would later become close friends and hunting partners of Granville Calhoun, and all three were mentioned prominently in Horace Kephart's writings. The Cable clan was also well-known for its strain of Plott bear dogs, known in some circles as Cable-Plotts.

Joshua Calhoun opened a store to serve the community and his family prospered there. Hazel Creek proved to be a wonderful place for young Granville to hone his hunting and fishing skills. As an adult, Granville tried his hand at several vocations, including logging and railroading. But he eventually decided to follow his father into the business of being a merchant. It afforded him the opportunity to be his own boss, and to hunt and fish whenever he pleased.

Renowned bear hunter "Little John" Cable and one of his celebrated Cable/Plott dogs, early 1900s. *Courtesy of Great Smoky Mountains National Park Archives.*

There was nothing that Granville Calhoun enjoyed more than fishing and hunting. Writer John Parris recorded many of Granville's best outdoor stories in three of his books, *These Storied Mountains* (1972), *Mountain Bred* (1967) and *Roaming the Mountains* (1955). Much of the information that follows comes from those books or from interviews found in the Great Smoky Mountains National Park archives, as well as personal anecdotes from my childhood in Bryson City.

Granville described the hunting on Hazel Creek like this:

> *This was great hunting country in those days. A man could hunt just about anything and everything—bear, deer, squirrel and wild turkey. When I was young, folks that carried a rifle to get something for supper never came home a-suckin' the barrel. Back then the woods were full of turkeys. We ate turkey whenever we wanted one, but we probably only ate it once a month or so, as we were more fond of squirrels. We ate groundhog in the spring of the year and coon and venison and bear in the wintertime. We shifted from one kind of meat to another. There was plenty of game back then.*

Though Granville did not eat turkey often, he truly loved to turkey hunt and there were plenty of them. He once counted over two hundred turkeys on a four-mile stretch above Hazel Creek between Locust Ridge and Proctor Ridge. Calhoun recalled to Paris, "In my time I killed many a turkey. I used an old Winchester rifle. They were big turkeys back then. Sometimes we'd camp and roast them over a fire. They are awful good that way. I was a good turkey caller. I always called them in with my mouth, I never used an artificial caller."

As in most Smoky Mountain communities, Hazel Creek hunters often gathered for shooting matches. Sometimes they would shoot targets, but more often they would have "live" turkey shoots. Granville described them this way: "Back then we'd have real live turkey shoots. We'd cut a hole in the top of a box and put a live turkey in there, with his head and neck sticking out of the box and we'd shoot it off. Come fall of the year we had a turkey shoot almost every Saturday down at Proctor." However, Calhoun did not see much sport in this himself and he added, "I didn't go in too much for the turkey shoots. I liked to do my turkey shooting out in the woods where they weren't boxed up."

Granville was a skilled angler and used a simple cane pole with a horsehair line that he made himself. Calhoun stated that "nothing can beat a horsehair line, it won't tangle in the bushes or get caught." Trout in the Hazel Creek watershed had never seen a hatchery. They were truly native fish. Granville referred to them as speckled or brook trout, while many old-timers referred to them simply as "specks." Calhoun said that the forebears of these fish were in the Smokies well before the first Indian had ever settled there.

He remembered the *average*-sized trout back then as being eight to ten inches long, and he stated that he had often caught them up to sixteen inches in length. Granville and his brother-in-law Jud Hall had a fishing contest on Proctor Creek in the summer of 1898. They set a time limit of eleven hours, and on that sunny Saturday Calhoun said that he caught almost a fish a minute until "my arm wore out and I quit," but he added that Jud continued to fish a few hours longer. Their final total was Jud with 237 trout and Granville, the winner, with 239.

Calhoun said that after the contest they gave all their neighbors "a good mess of fish and kept plenty for ourselves." He concluded, "It would take an army of men, fishing day and night to have caught them all. We went back to the same place a week later and you couldn't even tell that it had ever been fished."

Granville Calhoun was a fine all-around sportsman, but bear hunting was undoubtedly his favorite sport, and it was what he was probably best known for. Granville fondly recalled:

> *The best bear hunting there ever was, was back there in the Smokies on Hazel Creek and the country beyond. Once I killed three bear on a single hunt. They were big bear then. I killed one that weighed over 600 pounds. Some said it was the largest bear ever killed in the Smokies. I don't know. But I do know that the scales wouldn't weigh it. The scales we had only drug five hundred pounds and the scales hit the top mark and almost broke.*

Bear hunting was a sport that Granville not only enjoyed, but one that he respected. He understood well the dangers and rigors of this strenuous sport. It was a sport in which a man could easily be killed by animals, another hunter, the elements or the land itself. For those reasons, Calhoun felt that liquor and hunting were a dangerous combination. Anyone who hunted with him was strictly forbidden to drink on the hunt. Or as he put it, "If we found a feller with a jug in the woods we sent him packing or else made him stay at the cabin."

Calhoun knew the land intimately and he understood that a man could easily get lost and die in one of the many laurel thickets or "hells" that covered the mountainsides. A friend of Granville's from Forney Creek named Irving Huggins was once lost in a laurel jungle for six days. He nearly starved to death before finally finding his way out. This five-hundred-acre tract of twisted laurel between Bone Valley and the main fork of Hazel Creek was thereafter referred to as "Huggins' Hell." Calhoun said, "A man could get lost in there and starve to death, it wasn't called Huggins' Hell for nothing. There are other laurel hells in the Smokies, but this one is a real devil's nest. It's impossible to walk through and difficult to crawl."

Perhaps the danger of it all was part of the allure of the hunt. Regardless of the specific reasons, Granville Calhoun dearly loved to bear hunt, and he hunted regularly until he was more than eighty years old. Granville remembered one of the most successful bear hunts that he was ever on. But it was a hunt in which, oddly enough, only one bear was killed. He and his father-in-law, Crate Hall, were looking for lost cattle when they met eight bear hunters at the Hall Cabin near the Tennessee state line. The Hall and Spence cabins were both old herders' cabins located on Thunderhead Mountain, and they were both legendary base camps for local hunters.

Calhoun and Hall agreed that they wanted to hunt with the group, but they all decided to first get in a store of food before leaving on the long bear hunt. The next morning the men left the cabin in separate directions with the plan that they would all kill something to eat and return to the cabin before dark.

Hunters and Plott hound at the famous Spence Field hunting cabin in 1924. *Courtesy of Great Smoky Mountains National Park Archives.*

Hall cabin, legendary hunting shelter on Thunderhead Mountain, 1919. *Courtesy of Great Smoky Mountains National Park Archives.*

Granville killed six turkeys, all weighing between sixteen and twenty pounds each, and he barely managed to carry them all back to the cabin. As the sun began to set, the other nine hunters returned back to the cabin loaded with game. Calhoun exclaimed in amazement, "We had the biggest bunch of game that I ever saw brought in at one time. We had eleven turkeys, a dozen squirrels, a whole raft of pheasants, a bear, a deer, a groundhog and a coon."

The party enjoyed a wilderness feast for their supper as they excitedly looked forward to a good bear hunt the next day. Granville continued his story:

> *The next morning we set out, some of the fellers had dogs and we looked forward to a good bear fight. But the joke was on us that day. We never saw a single bear or even heard one in the brush. We didn't kill a thing. I reckon word got passed around among the bear and other animals that a bunch of true shooters was in the mountains and they all high-tailed it for parts unknown and holed in.*

Calhoun maintained that he once killed the oldest bear ever to have lived in the Great Smokies. He recounted the story to John Paris:

> *This bear I am telling you about was the oldest bear ever killed in the Smokies, I reckon it was forty years old. Don't you want to know how I knew the bear was that old? Well, I didn't when I killed it, though I knew*

117

Swain County hunters on Hazel Creek, circa 1920s. Standing second from left is Mark Cathey. Standing fifth from left is Granville Calhoun. *Courtesy of Jim Casada.*

that it had been here a long time. There wasn't no way that I knew of that I could rightly figure its age. How I found out is the story, but I've got to go back a ways.

The Squire of Hazel Creek paused before continuing:

Back at the time of the Civil War, old man Dewitt Gormerly started out from the valley with a wagon load of apples. Well, now, he had a pet bear that he always took along to show off and help sell his apples. This particular time he was going with a load of apples over to Maryville. He had the bear in a wooden cage that he had made. Just as he reached the top of the mountains his steers stalled and stumbled. They lost their footing and the wagon started to roll back down the mountain. It bounced into a tree, spilling apples, and dumping the bear cage. The cage broke open and the bear jumped out and headed into the timber. That was the last old man Gormerly saw of his bear.

Well, about forty years later, my father sent word to me one day that if I wanted a bear fight to come on up to his house. I got my rifle and my dogs and I went up there.

Upon arriving at his father's house, he found signs that a large bear had been ravaging the apple orchard. The bear returned that night. Granville's bear dogs struck its trail and the race was on. They chased the bruin for more than five miles before the dogs finally bayed the bear and Calhoun killed it.

Recalling the appearance of the dead rogue bear, he stated:

That was the raggedist bear I ever saw. Its coat looked like hog fur. Its ears were marked, just like you mark cattle to tell they're yours. The teeth were worn down to the gums. Reckon that was why he was so poorly. Didn't have no teeth to eat with. But he was a big bear, anyhow. Measured nine feet from nose to tail. He was a master brute and would have chawed them dogs up if he'd had any teeth.

A few days later Calhoun was talking to Matt Taylor in Bryson City, telling him about the huge old bear and its unusual ear markings. Taylor smiled and told Granville that he was familiar with the ear marks. They were the same marks that Dewitt Gormerly had used to identify his pet bear, the one that had escaped forty years earlier en route to Maryville, Tennessee.

The ancient bruin, however, had the last laugh. Granville said that even after cooking the old bear for three days the meat was still unfit to eat and he added, "That bear was shore tough when we tried to eat it. A man might as well have tried to gnaw shoe leather."

This bear is most likely the same bruin that Horace Kephart referred to as Old Reelfoot in his 1913 book *Our Southern Highlanders*. The description of the bear, as well as the fact that he indicates that Granville made the kill, further verifies the probability of this.

Life was good for Granville Calhoun on Hazel Creek. Not only was he respected as a great bear hunter but also as a savvy and honest businessman. He expanded his business holdings to include real estate, a post office and the first movie theatre in Proctor. But by the early 1900s, things were starting to change—for the worse. First came an influx of large lumber companies, followed later by the National Park Service and the Tennessee Valley Authority, all of which dramatically affected the valley. Granville sadly remembered, "Then came the lumbermen. Why, it was just like a revolution and I guess it was. It changed the valley. Folks who understood a rifle trigger and a fishing pole saw things that they had never heard of, much less seen. There wasn't much time left for hunting and fishing."

Though the Hazel Creek era as a sportsman's paradise was drawing to an end, Granville Calhoun would play a vital role in its closing chapters. And none was more important than the day in 1904 when he met an alcoholic, middle-aged librarian from St. Louis, Missouri, at the railroad depot in nearby Bushnell. Granville had been requested by a local mining official to pick up this visitor and show him around.

The stranger turned out to be Horace Kephart, a man who had deserted his wife and children in St. Louis to seek a life of solitude in the Great Smoky Mountains. Granville Calhoun was no braggart, but by his own admission over the next few years he taught Kephart everything that he knew about hunting, fishing and camping in the Great Smokies. Granville not only instructed Kephart in the art of woodcraft, but he introduced him to many other masters of the trade, men like Quill Rose, Little John Cable, Fonz Cable, Matt Hyde and Mark Cathey—all of whom Kephart often hunted and fished with.

Though Kephart was an alcoholic and a man with his own set of personal demons, he nevertheless proved to be a quick study in the sporting life of the

Horace Kephart at a hunting camp. *Courtesy of Great Smoky Mountains National Park Archives.*

Great Smokies. Thanks to the tutelage of Calhoun and his friends, Horace Kephart eventually became one of the most prolific outdoor writers of the first half of the twentieth century. Kephart wrote scores of articles for publications like *Forest and Stream*, *Sports Afield* and *Recreation*, among many others. But it was his 1906 field manual *Camping and Woodcraft* and his 1913 book *Our Southern Highlanders* for which Kephart is most famous. Both these classic works remain in print and are still popular today.

By 1946, Granville Calhoun's friend Horace Kephart had been dead for fifteen years and the National Park Service and the TVA had taken over all of Granville's property on Hazel Creek. His beautiful two-story home was being used for a ranger bunkhouse. However, he had reserved the right for one last bear hunt in the fall of 1946. At the age of seventy-one, he invited all of his hunting buddies for one last hurrah on Hazel Creek.

These Hazel Creek nimrods made the best of their last bear hunt. They ran sixteen bear and killed three their first day. The next day they shot two more bruins. Before their season was finished, twenty-seven bears had been harvested in the final bear hunt in the Hazel Creek watershed. Granville Calhoun moved to Bryson City shortly after that, and he continued to bear hunt in other parts of the mountains until he was eighty years old.

But things would never be the same for the old hunter. An era and a way of life in the Great Smokies had come to an end. Most of the places of his fondest memories were either underwater or were impossible or illegal to access. However, while his land could be taken away from him, Granville Calhoun's memories were his to cherish forever. And the Squire of Hazel Creek held fondly to them until his death in 1978 at the age of 103.

CHAPTER TEN

FULL CIRCLE

Our people can not live independently of the English. The Clothes we wear we can not make ourselves. We use their ammunition to kill deer. We can not make our own guns. Every necessity of life we must have from the white people.
—Cherokee Chief Skigunsta in a 1745 letter to the governor of South Carolina commenting on the loss of tribal hunting culture to the English

Well, it seems a good book. It is strange that the white people are no better after having had it so long.
—Cherokee Chief and renowned bear hunter Yonaguska, commenting on his opinion of the Christian Bible in the early 1800s

We had children and we were happy. I set my traps and caught or shot most any kind of game. We lived well. I paid a dollar an acre for this land. Now, just look at it! It's all fired messed up and these public works is doing it!
—Smoky Mountain hunter Abe Coggle speaking to Robert Mason around 1915 about big business loggers ruining his East Tennessee homelands

Water and wilderness swallowed them up, it made Swain County a poor county. The government was responsible. The government wiped them out.
—Granville Calhoun to John Parris in 1969 regarding the communities and hunting lands lost to the formation of Fontana Lake and the Great Smoky Mountains National Park

Four comments made centuries apart by two distinctively different—yet uniquely similar—hunting cultures, both lamenting an end to their way of life. Some would call it poetic justice that the concerns of twentieth-century white hunters were in many ways identical to those of their Cherokee counterparts from the eighteenth century. Call it what you will, things had definitely come full circle.

The golden age of hunting had come to an end in the mid-1900s, just as the Cherokee *duyuktv* or right way of life had two hundred years earlier in the mid-1700s. No longer could freeborn mountaineers roam the Great Smokies hunting and camping for days or weeks at a time wherever they wished. Never again will we see the likes of men who matched these mountains like John Denton, Quill Rose, Yonaguska, Mark Cathey, Bob Benge and all the other hunting legends of the Great Smokies.

But all was not lost. The next generation of mountain hunters, men like Taylor Crockett, Von Plott, Gola Ferguson, Dewey Sharp and others, became hunting legends in their own right. And they in turn passed the torch to a new generation of Southern mountain hunters, all of whom honor the tradition of their hunting forefathers and who perpetuate their legacy.

Sportsmen like Andy Blankenship, Wayne McCurry, Burdet Brinkley, Glen Braswell, John Jackson, Junior Keefer, Tommy Wilcox, Charles Brown, Jim Casada, Gerald Phillips, Rodney Burris and Roy Stiles, among others, still maintain and treasure their rights to hunt and fish in these storied mountains. More importantly, they are all committed to seeing these traditions preserved for generations to come. It is interesting to note, too, that if you look closely, you will find direct descendants of golden age legends like the Denton, Orr and Plott families still representing their sporting clans today.

These modern-day nimrods can even add a man hunter to their roster in Graham County native Marshall McClung. McClung is related to the legendary Lovin clan, so living in the woods came naturally to the lad, as he honed his woodcraft growing up in the small community of Atoah. As an adult, he worked twenty-seven years with the United States Forest Service and regularly attended tracking schools for federal law enforcement officers. Marshall was always the best student there and he soon rivaled even the instructors in his man hunting talents. McClung was soon named search and rescue team coordinator for the U.S. Forest Service and served in that capacity for the bulk of his career with them. He also has served as either assistant director or director of the Graham County Rescue Squad Search and Rescue team for more than twenty years.

With almost 200,000 acres of federal mountain woodlands in Graham County, there are ample opportunities for sportsmen and hikers to get lost or injured in this vast and rugged terrain. And as McClung told me with a smile in 2008, they almost always get hurt or lost in the worst sort of weather, making his job even more difficult.

Thomas "Tommy" Denton Wilcox and Plott hound. *Courtesy of Leota Wilcox.*

However, Marshall has proven to be well suited for the task—and for good reason. McClung looks upon his job as a ministry of sorts and he feels that it is his Christian obligation to provide solace for others. His first priority is to find the individual alive and bring him or her back to safety. But even if he can only find a dead body, McClung feels that he can at least bring some closure to the lost victim's family.

Over the past forty-one years, Marshall McClung has rescued or found at least forty people in the dense forests of Graham County. Unlike the man hunters of frontier times, McClung uses his man hunting skills only for the good of his fellow man. He is a fine example of mountain man hunting coming full circle—in a good way. McClung is also a fine writer who has published a book on Graham County history and writes a column for the *Graham County Star* newspaper.

Even in these modern times, the spirit of past Smoky Mountain hunting legends continues to flourish. While there is no doubt in my mind that these deceased old-timers would appreciate being remembered today, they would be prouder still to know that future hunting legends continue to be created. More importantly, they can rest assured in knowing that their hunting legacy will continue for generations to come in the Great Smoky Mountains.

And who knows? Maybe someday there will be a book written about these later-day nimrods too.

BIBLIOGRAPHY

Brewer, Carson, and Alberta Brewer. *Valley So Wild*. Knoxville: East Tennessee Historical Society, 1975.

Campbell, A.G. *Hunting the Wild Boar and Bear of Appalachia*. Tabor City, NC: Atlantic Publishing Company, 1985.

Coggins, Allen R. *Place Names of the Smokies*. Gatlinburg, TN: Great Smoky Mountains Natural History Association, 1999.

Davis, Donald Edward. *Where There Are Mountains*. Athens: University of Georgia Press, 2000.

Duncan, Barbara R., with Brett Riggs. *Cherokee Heritage Trails Guidebook*. Chapel Hill: University of North Carolina Press, 2003.

Dykeman, Wilma. *The French Broad*. New York: Rhinehart, 1955.

Ellison, George. "Mark Cathey." In *The Heritage of Swain County, N.C.* Edited by Hazel Jenkins. Winston Salem, NC: History Division of Hunter Publishing, 1988.

———. *Mountain Passages: Natural and Cultural History of Western North Carolina and the Great Smoky Mountains*. Charleston, SC: The History Press, 2005.

Ellison, George, and Elizabeth Ellison. *Blue Ridge Nature Journal: Reflections on the Appalachian Mountains in Essays and Art*. Charleston, SC: The History Press, 2006.

Evans, Raymond. "Bob Benge." *Journal of Cherokee Studies* 1, no. 2 (Fall 1976).

Fradkin, Arlene. *Cherokee Folk Zoology: The Animal World in Native American People 1700–1838*. New York: Garland, 1990.

Frome, Michael. *Strangers in High Places*. Knoxville: University of Tennessee Press, 1966.

Gasque, Jim. *Hunting and Fishing in the Great Smokies*. New York: Alford, 1947.

Bibliography

Hall, Joseph S. *Smoky Mountain Folks and Their Lore*. Asheville, NC: Published in Cooperation With the Great Smoky Mountains Natural History Association, 1960.

Hunnicutt, Samuel J. *Twenty Years of Hunting and Fishing in the Great Smoky Mountains*. Knoxville: S.B. Newman, 1926.

Kephart, Horace. *Our Southern Highlanders*. Knoxville: University of Tennessee Press, 1976.

King, Duane. "Cherokee Bows." *Journal of Cherokee Studies* 1, no. 2 (Fall 1976).

Mason, Robert L. *The Lure of the Great Smokies*. Boston: Houghton Mifflin Company, 1927.

McClung, Marshall. *Mountain People—Mountain Places*. Robbinsville, NC: Graham County Historical Association, 2006.

Medford, W. Clark. *The Early History of Haywood County*. Asheville, NC: Miller Printing Company, 1961.

Mooney, James. *Myths of the Cherokee and Sacred Formulas of the Cherokees*. Nashville: Charles and Randy Elder Publishing, 1982.

Parris, John. *Mountain Bred*. Raleigh, NC: Edwards and Broughton Company, 1967.

————. *Roaming the Mountains*. Raleigh, NC: Edwards and Broughton Company, 1955.

————. *These Storied Mountains*. Raleigh, NC: Edwards and Broughton, 1972.

Plott, Bob. *Strike & Stay: The Story of the Plott Hound*. Charleston, SC: The History Press, 2007.

Powell, William S. *The North Carolina Gazetteer: A Dictionary of Tar Heel Places*. Chapel Hill: University of North Carolina Press, 1968.

Powers, Elizabeth, with Mark Hannah. *Cataloochee, Lost Settlement of the Smokies*. Charleston, SC: Powers-Hannah, 1982.

Rozema, Vicki. *Footsteps of the Cherokee*. Winston Salem, NC: John F. Blair, 1995.

Strutin, Michael. *History Hikes of the Smokies*. Gatlinburg, TN: Great Smoky Mountain Natural History Association, 2003.

Timberlake, Henry. *The Memoirs of Lt. Henry Timberlake*. Cherokee, NC: Museum of Cherokee Indian Press, 2007.

Wiggonton, Elliot. *Foxfire Five*. Garden City, NY: Anchor Books, 1979.

Zeigler, Wilbur G., and Ben Grosscup. *The Heart of the Alleghanies or Western North Carolina*. Raleigh, NC: Alfred Williams, 1883.

About the Author

B ob Plott is the great-great-great-grandson of Johannes Plott, who first brought the Plott bear hounds to America in 1750. He has spent most of his professional career working either as a manufacturing manager or a martial arts instructor. He is an avid outdoorsman and an accomplished woodcarver and sketch artist. Bob is a member of the American Plott Association, the National Plott Hound Association and the North Carolina Bear Hunters Association. This is his second book. He lives with his wife, son and their Plott hounds outside of Statesville, North Carolina.

Visit us at
www.historypress.net